To

Dunc

from Ann + Lesley.

"Happy father's Day."

CO-031

ROTTWEILERS

Champion Graudstark's Rhapsody, owned by Virginia Koerber. Rottweilers are among the most popular dog breeds available today.

BEST OF BREED
OR VARIETY
HENDERSONVILLE
KENNEL CLUB
APRIL 1982
PHOTO BY SABRINA

Front endpapers: Show-quality Rottweilers are bred for their conformation, or how well they measure up to their breed standard of perfection.

ROTTWEILERS

All the information you need about selecting and keeping a Rottweiler—featuring sections on the breed's history, training, health care, breeding, and showing.

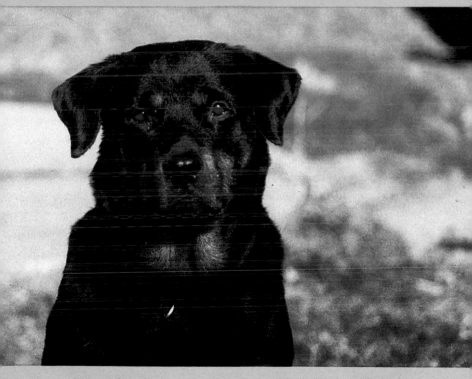

Am. and Can. Ch. Von Gailingen's Dassie Did It, U.D.T., Can. C.D., owned by Catherine Thompson, Freehold, New Jersey.

——Anna Katherine Nicholas——

© 1987 by T.F.H. Publications, Inc.

Distributed in the UNITED STATES by T.F.H. Publications, Inc., 211 West Sylvania Avenue, Neptune City, NJ 07753; in CANADA to the Pet Trade by H & L Pet Supplies Inc., 27 Kingston Crescent, Kitchener, Ontario N2B 2T6; Rolf C. Hagen Ltd., 3225 Sartelon Street, Montreal 382 Quebec; in CANADA to the Book Trade by Macmillan of Canada (A Division of Canada Publishing Corporation), 164 Commander Boulevard, Agincourt, Ontario M1S 3C7; in ENGLAND by T.F.H. Publications Limited, 4 Kier Park, Ascot, Berkshire SL5 7DS; in AUSTRALIA AND THE SOUTH PACIFIC by T.F.H. (Australia) Pty. Ltd., Box 149, Brookvale 2100 N.S.W., Australia; in NEW ZEALAND by Ross Haines & Son, Ltd., 18 Monmouth Street, Grey Lynn, Auckland 2 New Zealand; in SINGAPORE AND MALAYSIA by MPH Distributors (S) Pte., Ltd., 601 Sims Drive, #03/07/21, Singapore 1438; in the PHILIPPINES by Bio-Research, 5 Lippay Street, San Lorenzo Village, Makati Rizal; in SOUTH AFRICA by Multipet Pty. Ltd., 30 Turners Avenue, Durban 4001. Published by T.F.H. Publications Inc. Manufactured in the United States of America by T.F.H. Publications, Inc.

Contents

Introducing the Rottweiler

It is most foolish to add a dog to one's family without first learning everything you possibly can about the breed you've selected. The "doggie in the window" concept can be disasterously misleading if you picture the animal as remaining forever as it is then, without stopping to consider the almost daily changes which occur between the time a dog is a young puppy and the day he becomes a fully mature dog. These changes in size and temperament create a vastly different situation regarding the suitability of a particular breed of dog for your home and way of life.

Rotties get along well with other animals. These friends all belong to Al and Bonnie Wimberly of Florida.

Always bear in mind that it is the *mature* dog you will have, hopefully, as a family member for a dozen or more years, so think before you buy.

CHARACTER AND VERSATILITY

In choosing a dog, one needs an awareness of the special characteristics associated with fully grown members of the breed he or she represents. Rottweilers are adorable puppies: cute, small, and cuddly when you first own them. But they will become extremely powerful, muscular, and strong dogs of a height measuring between 22″ to 25″ if females and 24″ to 27″ if males by the time they have become full grown. These are power-packed inches as well, Rottweilers being heavily boned, muscular, and strong. Be sure that you are aware of this when you are tempted to bring home the puppy and that you will be able to cope with and enjoy so much dog, as one finds in these magnificent animals.

Being very special dogs, Rottweilers do not just automatically prove to be ideal for any type of home and family. They are loyal, devoted dogs who form strong attachments to their owner and their surroundings. This makes them natural protectors, but it also makes them demanding of your time and attention. The companionship of your presence is their greatest joy; at home, in the car, visiting, or no matter what the circumstances, your Rottweiler basks in being with you. Thus if you have little time to spend with your dog, and a full schedule of interests which cannot include him, perhaps a less demanding breed might work full potential. The feeling of a strong bond of affection, devotion, and sharing with his folks or special person is the way of life under which these

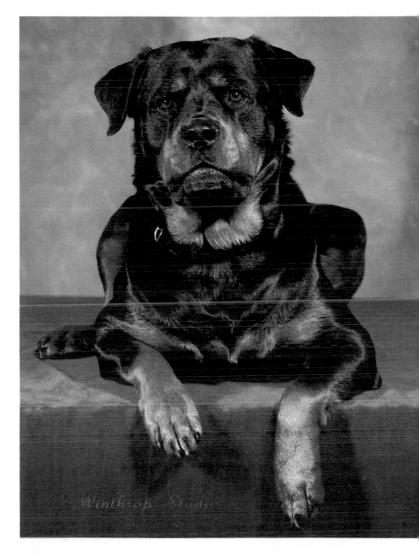

out more satisfactorily. A Rottweiler who is ignored and receives little of his owner's attention never does attain his

Ch. Doroh's Fantastic Serenade, Am. and Can. C.D.X., owned by Peter and Marilyn Piusz of New York.

dogs flourish to become truly representative of the finest in the breed.

Rottweilers are widely admired for their handsome, dignified, and noble demeanor. The very sight of one demands respect and admiration. They serve as efficient, fearless, and reliable guard dogs; as playmates for the children who not only *play* with them but *guard* them as well; and as companionable, sensible, and, yes, even *amusing* members of your household. Rottweiler owners delight in exchanging stories of their dogs, many being very much the clown at heart when relaxed and with the family, seeming to have an almost human sense of humor. Very definitely this breed is made up of "people dogs," basking in human companionship. The ideal life for a member of this breed is in the role of "family dog."

The owner of a Rottweiler must be a *responsible* person qualified to share life with this breed. The overlooking of this fact can cause much grief, as I shall point out. But prior to doing so I must comment that everything of value in life has its price, and Rottie owners of my acquaintance obviously feel that the special care and attention involved is well worthwhile. Socialization is very important in cultivating the best personality traits in a Rottweiler. Pups need to be handled and played with frequently.

TRAINING IS A MUST

In the case of the Rottweilers, the list of owner responsibilities starts with a very complete and careful course in obedience training for the dog. This should start when your puppy is about three months old and should continue until he has reached the point of reliable compliance *immediately* upon receiving your commands. So large and power-packed a dog *must* be completely obedient instantly upon the sound of your voice. Since these are among the most intelligent of dogs, it is not all that difficult to achieve this; but it must be done conscientiously and thoroughly. An untrained Rottie over whom no one has control can become a menace to himself and to the neighborhood. Start him off at home as soon as he is three months old, keeping the sessions short (ten minutes or so at a time) and making a

Australia has produced and imported some fine Rottweilers, among which include Aust. Ch. Zeldermann Zuleika (facing page top and middle), owned by Ebshine Kennels, and Aust. Ch. Rottser Valeda, C.D., pictured with Aust. Ch. Brabantsia Delrego as a puppy (bottom). Stephen Lodge, owner.

game of it with lots of praise, a treat when directions are correctly followed, and petting. Work initially on the basics. "Come," "sit," "stay," "heel," and "down" are early lessons which the two of you can work out together until the puppy reaches six months age, when the two of you should enroll in an obedience training class (which you can locate through the breeder of your puppy or through your veterinarian). Your attention to this training is the basis of all good people-Rottweiler public relations. Here, again, you will need to spend *time* with your dog. You may well find yourself becoming so interested in the obedience work with your dog that you will want to try him out in obedience competition at the trials, working for a Companion Dog degree (C.D.), from which the next step is Companion Dog Excellent (C.D.X.), then a Utility Dog (U.D.), possibly Tracking Dog (T.D.), and perhaps even eventually that grandest of all titles, Obedience Trial Champion (O.T.Ch.). A booklet describing the rules and regulations of A.K.C.

Ch. Doroh's Jaegerin v Noblehaus (top) at seven weeks old, owned by Mark and Patricia Schwartz, New York. Ch. Brimstone Bold Whisper, TT (bottom), owned by Brimstone Kennels and Pat Cyr.

obedience trial competition is available, free of charge for single copies, from the American Kennel Club, 51 Madison Avenue, New York, New York 10010. But remember that, whether or not you ever decide to try your hand at competitive obedience, a Rottweiler *must* have the advantage of a thorough obedience

accept your friends into your home," adding the advice that in case you are planning to be away, or for any reason plan to leave the dog in the care of others, "people expected to be in contact with the dog during your absence should be thoroughly familiar with it." This is quite true. For although Rottweilers are not senseless biters, and are slow

Fifteen-month-old Hertzog Astro, sired by Aust. Ch. Retohr Regnans out of the dam Aust. Ch. Rotvel Uberbeiten. Owned by Cheryl Wakeham, Australia.

education in order to live as a good citizen in a family and neighborhood situation.

In the words of the American Rottweiler Club in one of their pamphlets on the breed, "Your Rottweiler must be carefully schooled to

to actually bite without what they consider to be provocation, it should be remembered that through generation after generation the ancestors of our modern Rottweiler have been trained as guard dogs, their protective instinct having been cultivated and nurtured to the utmost. Thus the guard dog instinct is there right behind your dog waiting to surface. This is a possessive dog who takes his home, family, and all things belonging to the latter very much to heart and is liable to act should he feel they are being threatened. This instinct *must* be offset by good training and it must be under control at all times if problems are to be avoided. After all, even though someone may not actually be bitten, you will find hot resentment from anyone being cornered or herded by your Rottweiler when such person is a visitor or on your premises for legitimate reasons. Thus this instinct must be carefully channelled through obedience training as stated; and people who come to your home regularly either to visit you or for the purposes of working there or making deliveries should be "introduced" to the dog under your supervision as you make it abundantly clear that these are *friends* and permitted access to your house or grounds. Again, this involves the expenditure of some time; but how much better that is than just letting nature take its course and perhaps finding yourself isolated with no one willing to brave the dog on your property!

The other essential to responsible dog ownership, especially true when the dog is large and powerful as is a Rottweiler, is the installation of a fenced area in which the dog can safely enjoy being outdoors. Not a makeshift amateur-type enclosure, which a Rottie will be out of

before you know it, but a properly installed chain-link or woden fence which will keep him inside. If the dog is a "digger," add to this a row of railroad ties or cement blocks inside of and against the bottom of the fence to decrease his chances of digging out when you may not be noticing. Everyone who owns a dog should provide this protection for them. How many canine tragedies would be averted if they did so!

GETTING ALONG WITH CHILDREN

Characteristically, Rottweilers love children on whom their protective instincts seem to naturally center. Of course, as with all breeds, one sometimes meets an individual who is *not* fond of children and from whom they should be kept away, but generally it will be found that such a Rottweiler either has never become acquainted with a child or lives in a

If raised together from an early age, Rottweilers and children can become the best of friends, as evidenced by Faustus von Stolzenfels and Joshua Bo Johnson (facing page top) and Demon von Fox with her pal Matthew Fox (middle). These two Rottie youngsters (bottom) are owned by Edith Alphin, Altar Rottweilers, North Carolina.

childless household—or that he has been mauled or otherwise mistreated by one. As a parent, it is up to you to raise your children with the realization that animals are *not* to be hurt, played with too roughly, or treated unkindly. And until you know by observation that they have become friends, make certain that other people's children behave likewise with your dog. Do not allow children to abuse the dog under the heading of "play."

The ideal arrangement on which to base the perfect child-Rottweiler relationship is to raise the puppy with your youngster, either from babyhood or from the time you feel your child is ready for a pet. This is the best basis of all for a child-canine relationship and is an experience no one should miss as part of growing up. Their shared babyhood leads to true devotion between them which will last throughout the dog's lifetime and leave treasured memories as the child becomes an adult.

People sometimes wonder about the success of keeping other kinds of pets along with a Rottweiler. To the best of my knowledge, with sensible handling this causes no problem. Again, the younger at which the association begins, the more smoothly things should go; but I know of hundreds of Rottweilers and dogs of other breeds who

live contentedly together, as well as Rotties and cats. Why I know of one Rottweiler that is even friends with a pig!

ROTTWEILERS IN THE CITY

It is incorrect to feel that Rotties are unsuited to city or apartment living. On the contrary, they make out very well in this type of

16

These Rottweilers belong to one family. They are the progeny of Ch. Axel v Lerchenfeld, C.D.X., T.D.

Rottweiler in condition, but it will do the same for you, your figure, and your sense of well-being. In my opinion the Rottweiler is an ideal city dog, as this is one of the situations under which a dog with protective instincts is especially desirable and will add much to your safety and security. A carefully obedience-trained Rottweiler at your side will do much to guarantee your travelling the city streets in safety and to your apartment being considered out of bounds by burglars. Remember, though, you *must* ensure that your Rottie does get proper exercise, with at least one daily walk whereby he travels several blocks or more on lead with you, moving along at a fairly brisk rate of speed. This should be in addition, of course, to the three or four daily "trips to the curb," which often do not involve much more than that.

The need for walking your dog is not limited to city dwellers. Those whose dogs spend a goodly bit of time in a fenced yard also need to be taken for daily supervised walks, either on the lead or accompanied by the owner. In actual practice, dogs in a fenced area do *not* spend their time romping and playing for more than a very few moments, especially if out there alone. They check out the premises, look everything over, then sit down or lie down until something of

environment, especially if the owner provides at least one *real* walk daily. A good brisk walk will not only keep your

interest turns up.

Never turn your Rottweiler loose to roam the neighborhood by himself. A large dog is bound to cause neighborhood friction, as others may resent him on their premises and feel that their rights are being infringed upon. Actually no dog should be permitted to run at large. Too many misfortunes can befall an animal under those circumstances.

SCHUTZHUND

In Germany, Schutzhund training is a way of life for Rottweilers, and the gaining of the letters denoting Schutzhund training and degrees (SchH., SchH.I, II, and III) are of tremendous importance. In a way the requisites are similar to obedience degrees elsewhere, with the exception that a Schutzhund-trained dog is being trained as an attack dog. These titles are *not* officially recognized by the American Kennel Club, and Schutzhund work is not performed in the United States under A.K.C. jurisdiction. However, there are Rottie owners and Rottie trainers working in that field.

Rottweilers truly are a versatile breed as evidenced by these dogs who are participating in water retrieving (facing page top and middle) and by Ch. Marlo's Sohn v Axel, C.D., T.D. (bottom), owner-handled by Penny Dodds of California.

To the majority of us, it seems that Rotties have sufficient protective instincts to enable them to handle whatever situation may arise in normal

Ch. Koskemo Furst Hasso, SchH. III, FH, photographed in action during a protection exercise at the North American Schutzhund III Championship. Max and Pat Kaefer, owners.

family living. Unless the dog is being actually trained by experts for police work, most believe that the sharpening of these instincts is superfluous.

We could write indefinitely about the experiences of Rottweiler owners with their dogs, and the pleasure they enjoy through ownership of them. Their adaptability, companionship, intelligence, and disposition are sources of continual pleasure to those who live with them. As we have already stated, these are truly remarkable dogs.

19

Physical Attributes

In the preceding chapter, we told you of the temperament, adaptability, behavior patterns, and disposition of Rottweilers. To the layman, this translates into "character of the breed." But breed character means something else besides. To the breeder of pure-bred dogs, those who own them, show, and/or judge them, "character" also refers to the physical appearance of members of a breed, to the various features or combination of features which make these dogs distinctive from all others. This is known as "breed type."

When one thinks of a Rottweiler, one immediately envisions a heavily-boned, muscular, well-built animal standing 22" to 25" high at the withers (highest point of the shoulder) for bitches and 24" to 27" for dogs. Everything about a Rottie, as one looks at a member of the breed, should denote power and nobility.

Black in color with clearly defined rust markings, his compactness of build makes clear his strength and power

These handsome Rotties, owned by Noblehaus Rottweilers in New York, are raised as family members, not as kennel dogs. Pat and Mark Schwartz, owners.

with which he combines both endurance and agility. He is a substantial dog, reflecting the natural substance of the cart dog. A Rottweiler should never appear lightly built or overly refined, as this is atypical of the breed. The bitches as well as the dogs should reflect the "cart dog" influence of their early ancestors—rugged, "chesty," massively built, and muscular. Even though the bitches are smaller and should be distinctly feminine, they should not be undersized or "weedy" in appearance.

The Rottweiler should impress one as being a dog who clearly feels he owns the

world. Dignified, self-confident, aloof, and noble are the adjectives which immediately come to mind. From the front, one notes the massive chest, which extends to the elbow, and the heavily-boned straight forelegs ending in almost upright pasterns and round compact feet, the toes of which are well arched.

Still from the front, our eye travels again to the head where we note the well-placed ears set far apart on the skull to add to the appearance of the breadth of head. The ears are proportionately small and triangular in shape. The tip comes to about the mid-cheek area with the inner edge lying tightly against the cheek. Too long ears, or those set to low, are "houndy" in type and incorrect on a Rottweiler, while high-set ears also give an atypical expression to the Rottie—in this case terrier-like. Be aware that Rottie puppies go through various stages of ear carriage during the teething process. So do not panic at this time should the ears suddenly go haywire! It is permissible (and sensible, considering the importance of well-carried ears to the expression and general appearance of the grown Rottweiler) to tape a puppy's ears during the teething phase as an aid to correct carriage in the mature dog. If you are not familiar with how to do this, the breeder of your puppy should be willing to supply you with the information and, perhaps, if nearby, even demonstrate for you exactly how it should be done.

Nice head study of Ch. Pandemonium's Laredo v Blanka, owned by Valerie Cade and Mary Ellen Laycock of New York.

For ideal dentition, the Rottweiler should have a total of 42 teeth, of which 20 are in the upper jaw and 22 are in the lower jaw. They should be strong and correctly placed and they should meet in a scissors bite, which is one in which the tips of the lower incisors just touch the inside or the backs of the uppers. Anything other than a *correct*

scissors bite is to be penalized severely, this being true of a level bite or one that is twisted (wry).

Viewing the dog in profile, one notes the strength and length of the neck on which the noble head is proudly carried, the manner in which it strongly and gracefully arches to carry the head high. The firm topline, with no sign of a dip either while the animal is standing or moving, is straight from withers to croup. This is of importance, as a dog either high in rear or sloping in topline lacks the power to furnish the driving rear and far-reaching forequarter movement which is demanded of the breed. The loin is well muscled, deep and short. The croup, slightly sloping, should have breadth and be of medium length. A Rottweiler with a proper set on of tail cannot be too steep in croup. Correctly, the tail appears as an elongation of the topline of the dog, carried sometimes slightly arched when the dog is excited.

Forelegs and elbows are set well under the dog, which adds to the chesty impression. Hindquarters are strong, powerful, muscular, with good bend of stifle, the hock straight from joint to ground. Such hindquarters move powerfully and enable the Rottie to cover the ground well when he is in action. Rottweilers should be moved in the show ring at a trot, their natural gait, with obvious reach of front and drive of rear. In trotting, the dog moves with coordination, the back holding firm. As speed increases, the legs will present on the neck and thighs, but not to the extent of showing through the outer coat.

In showing a Rottweiler,

converge under his body toward the center line. Forelegs and hindlegs both should move directly ahead, the Rottweiler throwing them neither in nor out.

A Rottweiler coat is partially a double coat. The outer layer is straight and course, of medium length, and dense but flat lying. Beneath this is an undercoat

Winning Best of Breed and finishing his Canadian championship is Am. and Can. Ch. Hasso vom Steigstrassle, C.D. Michael Helmann, Illinois, owner.

one does so with the dog in a natural condition, the only trimming being that of removing whiskers only if desired.

Origin of the Breed

The Rottweiler traces its earliest roots to the ancient Roman Empire where several different types of dog were used for working purposes, among them a bristle-coated black dog whose principal occupation was herding. So strongly does the resemblance between these dogs and today's Rottweiler come through, that there can be little question in any student's mind that here is the original source of the dogs who later came to Germany, were developed there, and who became the progenitors of those wonderful dogs known as Rottweilers.

The first Rottweilers came to the Wurttemberg area of southern Germany as they accompanied the Roman invaders through Europe. These dogs were valuable to the invading troops for guarding and herding the cattle that served as the food supply and that, of necessity, had to be brought along "on the hoof" in those days prior to food preservatives and refrigeration. The dogs guarded the herd against loss, which was of vital importance to the success of these forays.

When the Roman troops left the area, some of their dogs remained behind in southern Germany where they and their offspring were quickly adopted as drover dogs by the butchers, farmers, and cattle dealers in the area of the important trading center known as Rottweil. These intelligent working dogs of great stamina and good "lasting ability" did not go unappreciated. They were needed not only for the transporting of the cattle (which sometimes travelled very considerable distances) but for the protection of the traders themselves. On the way to the market they helped to prevent loss of cattle. On the return trip home they were in charge of the money their owners had received in return for the cattle, assuring its safety from thieves. The money was transported in bags tied to the collars of these formidable dogs. Surely this was a much safer method than placing the money in the traders' hands should any encounters with would-be thieves take place.

Respect for the Rottweiler dogs increased as Rottweil grew from a trading center to a popular cultural headquarters. Before long, the "butcher's dogs" were arousing the interest of those visitors not formerly acquainted with them, which led to a lively demand to purchase some of these splendid dogs to take back home. In tribute to their acknowledged superiority over other dogs of the area, the Roman drover dogs became the Rottweiler dogs— to associate them forever more with the area in which they had become so admired and respected. That is how it happened that the original Roman drover dogs were bred and developed into Rottweilers by the Germans.

It took no time at all for competition to arise between those raising Rottweilers as to which owners might actually possess the best of all of

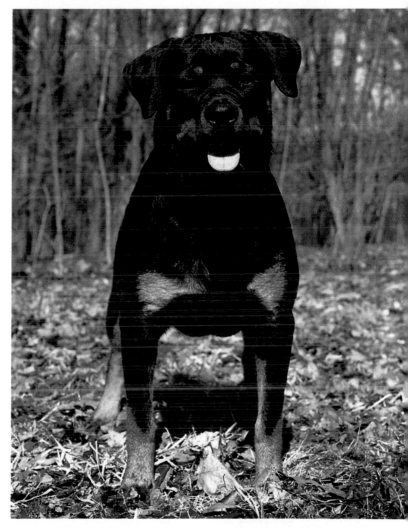

This ten-month-old, Ch. Pioneer's Beguiled, grew up to become the breed's first all-breed Best in Show bitch in the U.S. Virginia Aceti and Sheryl Hedrick, owners.

them. And just as is the case now, a dog particularly outstanding in looks, temperament, and working ability could bring a highly respectable price.

Some of Srigo Kennels' finest, bred by Felicia Luburich.

The Rottweiler dogs had a second job in addition to herding, that of pulling the milk carts. The time arrived, unfortunately, when railroads and resulting regulations necessitated a different form of cattle transportation, and the job of pulling milk carts was transferred to donkeys rather than the dogs. Rottweilers, thus deprived of their principal occupations, suddenly were in a decline so far as their popularity was concerned. How fortunate for all of us who love and admire the breed today that there were some owners who retained their once so highly regarded dogs as guards for home and property, and who knows, perhaps even in those days when the principal interest in dogs was for their usefulness, some may have been kept for the pleasure of their company. Had this not been the case, we just might not have Rottweilers to enjoy today.

When interest in the breed finally came to life again, it was in northern Germany rather than in the Rottweil area. Incredible as it seems, we have been told that in 1905 only one Rottweiler was to be found in all of Rottweil.

PRESENT-DAY ROTTWEILERS

A renewed interest began in the early part of the twentieth century in Hamburg and was brought about by a sudden realization of the qualifications possessed by these dogs for police work, this discovery attributed to the Hamburg Police

Department. The first two dogs with which they worked, Max von der Stahlenberg and Flock von Hamburg, were so proficient that the breed was officially recognized in 1910 by the German Police Association as the fourth police-dog breed. The German Rottweiler Club (DRK) which had been founded in Heidelberg on January 13, 1907 became affiliated with this association. But soon after that came the establishment of a newer club, the South Germany Rottweiler Club, also in Heidelberg, this one on April 26, 1907. A third club soon followed, the International Rottweiler Club (IRK) which soon picked up the pieces of the South Germany Rottweiler Club.

Germany over the years has produced Rottweilers of fantastic quality, dogs and bitches who stand in the background of the finest Rotties in all parts of the world. Since the accomplished merging of the DRK and the IRK in 1921 when the groups became together the General German Rottweiler Club (Allgemeiner Deutscher Rottweiler Klub, or ADRK) and the combination of the two previous stud books into the ADRK Stud Book, first published in 1924, ADRK has retained control of the Rottweiler world in Germany. All Rottweiler breeding there is done under the direct supervision of the Head Breed Warden and Regional Breeding Supervisors who are dedicated people bearing a strong loyalty and responsibility to the aims and purposes of the ADRK. All Rottweiler breedings in Germany, if the puppies are to be eligible for registration, must be performed solely under the advice and approval of these people.

Judy Hoover with an armful of five-week-old Beaverbrook pups owned by Laura and Gary Brewton, Tennessee.

When England and when the United States turned their attention to introducing Rottweiler dogs to their respective countries, it was of course to Germany that they turned for foundation stock.

27

The earliest Rotties to arrive in Great Britain competed at Crufts Dog Show in 1937. The earliest in the United States would seem to have been imported from Germany in the late 1920's since they competed at Westminster during the 1930's.

Marshall, Donnaj Kennels, New Hampshire. Ironically, *the following day,* thus on the same weekend, Kato's older full brother (Champion Rodsden's Duke Du Trier) also gained his first all-breed Best in Show, this dog owned by Dr. and Mrs. Nelse O.

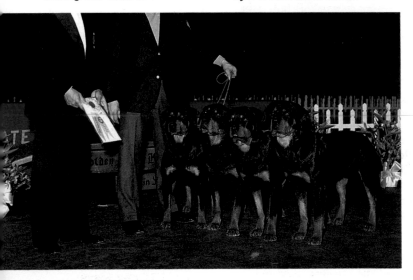

This is the first team of Rottweilers to go Best in Show with all dogs owned by the same owners, namely, Stephen and Charlotte Johnson of Washington.

It was not until May 28, 1971 that a Rottweiler won the first Best in Show, all-breeds, for the breed in the United States. This was Champion Rodsden's Kato v Donnaj, C.D.X., T.D., who had gained titular honors in both the United States and Canada previous to then and who gained this grand award owner-handled by Mrs. Janet

Olson of Bremerton, Washington and handled by Richard Orseno. These two first American Best-in-Show dogs were bred in the United States but of imported stock, their breeder having been Laura Coonley of Wheaton, Illinois. Their parents were Champion Rodsden's Kluge von der Harque, C.D. and Champion Franzl vom Kursaal.

Next came Duke's son, Champion Duke's Derek v Altmeister, to stand in the Best in Show circle, handled, as had been his sire, by Richard Orseno. Champion

Shearwater's Cochise followed, handled by Alan Levine for Shearwater Kennels. Then the fifth, in 1975, a German import named Champion Arno v Ingenhoe, owned by the Hills and handled by Kim Knoblock.

Champion Donnaj Vt. Yankee of Paulus, C.D.X. was the sixth U.S.A. Best in Show Rottie, the honor coming in June 1979. This dog, like Kato, was owned by Janet Marshall and he was Kato's grandson, bred by Pauline Rakowski and handled by Mel Goldman. Then in July 1979, the seventh Best-in-Show-winning Rottweiler came forth in Champion Rodsden's Bruin v Hungerbuhl, C.D. This dog gained the Best in Show rosette on five occasions, handled by Brian Martin for Jeffrey and Geraldine Kittner. A Dutch import, Champion Oscar van het Brabantpark was next to join those honored by Best in Show, this one handled by Corky Vroom for owners Clara Hurley and Michael Grossman.

Currently, numerous Rottweilers of great beauty and quality are winning Best in Show in all parts of the United States.

The International Federation for Rottweiler Friends (IRF) was founded in 1968, the idea having been conceived and the groundwork performed by the ADRK. This is a worldwide organization created for the purpose of cementing relationships between Rottweiler breeders in all parts of the world. Meetings are held every few years for the purpose of establishing common goals among all Rottweiler breeders, thus helping to assure the continued well-being and

A winner of the Dog World *Award of Canine Distinction, Ch. Radio Ranch Ebony Gold Bar. Marge Gold, owner.*

progress of the Rottweiler breed. Delegates are sent from specialty clubs throughout Europe and the United States to these gatherings where they are thus afforded the opportunity of meeting and discussing the breed and its future with delegates from the ADRK.

EARLY GREAT BRITAIN

We have already mentioned that Rottweilers appeared for the first time in the British show ring during 1937. These were owned by Mrs. Thelma

Gray, a lady successfully active in numerous breeds. It was her German import, Rozavel Arnolf v. d. Eichener Ruine, who was entered at Crufts that year; and he was one of the two belonging to Mrs. Gray at the time, the other having been International Champion Rozavel Vefa v Kohlerwald. A homebred of Mrs. Gray's, "Anna" became noted for outstanding success in obedience trials.

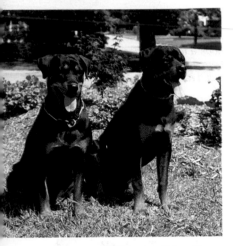

Hasso and Hilde von Schwabing, owned by Roy and Fran Hiltermann of Von Schwabing Kennels.

The intervention of World War II interrupted what was starting to be a brisk popularity rise for Rottweilers in Great Britain. However, interest again started up in 1954 when several German-born entries came to Mrs. Chadwick's kennel and when Ajax v Fuhrenhamp was representing Captain Roy-Smith at the dog shows.

EARLY CANADA
Present-day Rottweiler activity in Canada, now widespread, first started during the 1960's with Northwind Kennels, so highly influential in both United States and Canadian breeding programs. Patricia Hickman Clark, owner of this establishment, was as well the founder and first President of the parent specialty club for Rottweilers in Canada. Dogs and bitches from this kennel have produced a long line of famous champions, who in turn have begat outstanding producers.

Canada's first Best-in-Show-winning, all-breeds, Rottweiler was Canadian Champion Rintelma the Dragoon, also a leading winner of specialty shows, who was owned and bred by Pat Johnson and Jim Schwartz of Winnipeg.

AUSTRALIA
Australia has a very strong nucleus of Rottweiler breeding kennels and is fortunate in two really active specialty clubs, the Rottweiler Club of New South Wales and the Rottweiler Club of Victoria. Numerous breeders here are producing successful winning Rottweilers, and the breed is well loved by the Australian people.

Enjoying Your Rottweiler

Rottweiler owners are fortunate in that the breed is sponsored by a number of truly active and involved specialty clubs who are ready, willing, and anxious to encourage interest in and knowledge of the breed. Membership in one of these organizations can be very helpful and can add, both through information and sociability, to the fun you may enjoy as a Rottweiler owner.

The American Rottweiler Club issues a free pamphlet, in return for a stamped, self-addressed envelope (legal size), which contains useful information for the new or prospective Rottweiler owner. The pamphlet is available upon request from Doris Baldwin, P.O. Box 23741, Pleasant Hill, California 94523, who will also gladly supply any further information requested in connection with the breed.

There is also the Medallion

Rottweilers were used as cart dogs a few centuries ago, and here a pair of present-day Rotties pull a replica of one of the Seattle fire department's aerial ladder trucks.

Rottweiler Club in the Midwest, which was founded in 1959. The Colonial Rottweiler Club, for fanciers in the Mid-Atlantic States, recently sponsored its 26th Annual Specialty Show, this time in conjunction with Bucks County Kennel Club. Golden State Rottweiler Club, a highly active organization on the Pacific Coast since 1962, publishes *The Guardian Newletter of the Golden State Rottweiler Club,* which is circulated among hundreds of members and subscribers throughout the world.

The Western Rottweiler Club, founded in October 1962, has also done well for the breed, and, if still available, their booklet "On

Owning a Rottweiler" is an educational one.

The Dogwood Rottweiler Club is in the Atlanta, Georgia area and is a busy organization with a full program of Working-Group matches, all-breed matches, show-training classes, and all-breed obedience classes— plus Schutzhund and Tracking competition.

The newest of the Rottweiler specialty clubs is that of the Greater New York area. Although new, they have held a Rottweiler Symposium, Temperament Testing Society Tests, monthly obedience classes, and numerous other projects.

A WORD ABOUT HIP DYSPLASIA

There is no question that the most serious physical problem to have plagued the Rottweiler over the years has been hip dysplasia. In the beginning it was difficult to find a Rottie strain or bloodline clear of it. Rottweiler breeders decided that something must be done about this heartbreaking problem and proceeded accordingly.

There is a most impressive organization known as the Orthopedic Foundation for Animals, Inc. (O.F.A.), which is affiliated with the School of Veterinary Medicine at the University of Missouri, Columbia, Missouri. This is a non-profit organization formed for the purpose of collating and disseminating information concerning orthopedic diseases of animals, and it conducts the Dysplasia Control Registry. Dr. James S. Larsen is Project Director.

The organization advises, encourages, and establishes control programs to lower the incidence of orthopedic diseases; encourages and finances research in this field; and receives funds and issues grants to carry out these objectives.

To the Hip Dysplasia Control Registry X-rays may be sent for examination and certification. To have a Rottweiler certified, write to O.F.A. at the above address, and they will send you a packet free of charge in which you will find a 14" x 17" piece of film (Rottweiler size) along with a heavy backing sheet for use in returning the film in the same reusable envelope in which your packet arrived. The X-ray must include the entire pelvis down to and including the stifle joints. Instructions for proper positioning and other pertinent information will be included, along with an application card for identification of your dog. This information will become a permanent part of the X-ray film itself.

The Dog Show World

Quality in the sense of "show quality" is determined by various factors such as the dog's health, physical condition, temperament, ability to move, and appearance. Breeders trying to breed show dogs are attempting to produce animals which come as close as possible to the word description of perfection as set out in the breed standard.

Keep in mind that dog show terminology varies from one place to another and even from one time to another. If you plan to show your dog, it always makes sense to check with your local or national breed club or with the national dog registry for the most complete, most up-to-date information regarding dog show regulations. In Great Britain, for example, match shows are known as limit shows. Age limit also differs, as dogs less than six months old may not be shown in Britain. Additionally, Britain has no point system for dogs, rather the dogs compete for championship certificates (C.C.s). Thus, point shows are known as championship shows in Great Britain.

MATCH SHOWS

One of the best ways to see

Ch. Alina's Adelbear of Wesley winning one of his many Bests in Show, pictured at the same event that his great-grandsire won the breed's first Best in Show in the U.S. Photo courtesy of Jan Marshall, Vermont.

if your puppy has championship potential is to attend a match show which is usually organized by the local kennel club or breed specialty club. Such shows provide a useful learning experience for the amateur and they offer you the opportunity to see how well your dog measures up to others being shown. There you can mingle with owners and professional handlers and pick up basic guidelines in showmanship, performance, and procedure. You can learn a great deal merely by closely observing the professional handlers performing in the ring.

The age limit is usually reduced to two months at match shows so that puppies can have four months of training before they compete in the regular shows when they reach six months. This time also helps them to overcome any "crowd nervousness." As class categories are the same as those included at a regular show, much experience can be gained in this informal atmosphere. Entry fees are low and paid at the door.

You may want to invest in a grooming table if you plan to show your dog. The post adjusts to the height of your dog, while the loop fastens to his neck to keep him still.

Before you go to a show, your dog should be trained to gait at a trot beside you, with head up and in a straight line. In the ring you will have to gait around the edge with other dogs and then individually up and down the center runner. In addition, the dog must stand for examination by the judge, who will look at him closely and feel his head and body structure. He should be taught to stand squarely, hind feet slightly back and head up. He must hold the pose when you place his feet, and he must show a lively interest when you "bait" him, *i.e.,* tempt him with a piece of boiled liver or a small squeak toy.

There are all sorts of grooming products, available at most pet shops, that will help keep your dog's coat in top condition.

Check your dog's nails periodically; if they need to be trimmed, use a pet nail clipper.

If your puppy receives praise and words of encouragement from the judges and other knowledgeable people, then you can begin to dream of Westminster or Crufts. It is always useful to visit such prestigious shows to see the best examples of all the various breeds.

After you have taken some handling lessons yourself, or employed a professional handler, the next step is participation in the point shows where you can earn points toward your dog's championship.

POINT SHOWS

Unlike match shows where your dog was judged on ring behavior, at point shows he will be judged on conformation to his breed standard. It is advisable to write to your national dog

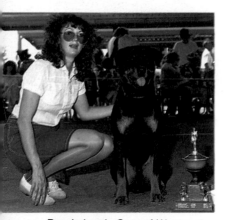

Powderhorn's Gero of Wencrest, C.D., Highest Scoring Rottweiler of the day at the Kennel Club of Pasadena–Golden State Rottweiler Club l2th Annual Specialty.

registry for information on how to register your dog and apply to dog shows. Below are the names and addresses of registries in the United States, Canada, Great Britain, and Australia.

The American Kennel Club
51 Madison Avenue
New York, NY 10010

The Canadian Kennel Club
111 Eglinton Avenue East
Toronto, Ontario M6S 4V7
Canada

The Kennel Club of Great Britain
1 Clarges Street
Piccadilly, London, W1Y 8AB, England

The Australian Kennel Club
Royal Show Grounds
Ascot Vale, Victoria, Australia

Your local kennel club can provide you with the names and addresses of the show-giving superintendents (or show secretaries) near you, who will be staging the club's dog show for them, and where you must write for an official entry form. The forms will be mailed in a pamphlet called the "premium list" which will include the names of the judges for each breed, a list of the prizes and trophies, the names and addresses of the show-giving club, where the show will be held, as well as the rules and required procedure. Make certain that you fill in the form clearly and carefully and mail it in plenty of time.

Before then, however, you will have to decide in which classes your dog should compete. In the United States these are: Puppy, Novice, Bred-by-Exhibitor, American-bred and Open.

Puppy Classes are for dogs six months of age and over but under twelve months which are not champions. The age of a dog shall be calculated up to and inclusive of the first day of the show.

The *Novice Class* is for dogs six months of age and over, whelped in the United States or Canada, which have not, prior to the official closing date for entries, won three first prizes in the Novice Class, a first prize in Bred-by-Exhibitor, American-bred or

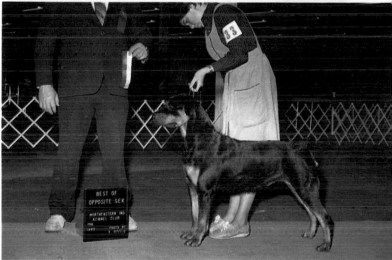

Ch. Artus v Adelshof, SchH. III (top) wins Best of Breed at the prestigious Westminster Kennel Club show in l985 for owner Alan Kruse, Michigan. Larry and Alice Lee, Indiana, own this lovely bitch, Ch. Baroness Elka von Dealcrest (bottom).

Open Class or one or more points toward championship. In Britain, of course, dogs competing in the Novice Class must have been whelped in Britain.

The *Bred-by-Exhibitor Class* is for dogs whelped in the U.S.A. or, if individually registered in the American Kennel Club Stud Book, for dogs in Canada that are six months of age and over. They must not be champions (although they may be in Britain), and must be owned wholly or in part by the person or the spouse of the person who was the breeder or one of the breeders of record. Dogs in this class must be handled by an owner or by a member of the immediate family of the owner. (This is not the case, however, in Britain.) Members of an immediate family for this purpose are: husband, wife, father, mother, son, daughter, brother and sister. This class has been referred to as the "breeder's showcase" as it is the one where the breeders can be justly proud of their achievements.

The *American-bred Class* is for all dogs (except champions) six months of age or over, whelped in the U.S.A. by reason of a mating that took place in the U.S.A.

The *Open Class* is for any dog six months of age or over, except in a member specialty club show held only for American-bred dogs, in which case the class is for American-bred dogs only.

In the United States and Canada, one does not enter the *Winners Class*. One earns the right to compete in it by

Kennels, or animal carriers, come in a number of sizes depending on the height and weight of your dog. These models are lightweight, easy to clean, and easy to carry.

winning first prize in one of the above classes. Winners Dog and Winners Bitch are the awards which carry points toward championship with them. Also designated by the judge are the Reserve Winners Dog and the Reserve Winners Bitch (in Britain these are designated Reserve C.C. Dog and Reserve C.C. Bitch) but they do not receive any points. This award means simply that the dog or bitch receiving it are standing "in reserve" should the Winners Dog or Winners Bitch be disallowed through any technicality in the official show rules and regulations.

The dog and bitch then compete against each other for Best of Winners, and they also vie with the champions in the Specials Class for Best of Breed and for Best of Opposite Sex to Best of Breed. In Britain, the Reserve C.C. winners compete against each other for Best of Breed, not Best of Winners.

Best of Breed is the highest-placing dog in a given breed, and that winner then represents the particular breed in Group competition. Groups include: Sporting Dogs, Herding Dogs, Hounds, Working Dogs, Terriers, Toys, and Non-sporting Dogs. The judge of each Group selects first, second, third, and fourth place among the Best of Breed winners within specific Groups. First-place winners in each Group then compete for

Electric nail groomers help smooth your dog's rough nail edges.

Best in Show.

A scale of points is printed in each dog-show catalog, and the number of points awarded in a breed depends on the number of dogs shown in competition. A win of three or more points at a show is called a "major." To attain championship, a dog must win a total of fifteen points under at least three different

Simply press each nail against the nail groomer and let the revolving dressing stone do the work.

judges, and included in those fifteen points must be two majors (each under a different judge). A dog that accumulates fifteen points and no majors does not qualify for championship. A dog must win in keen competition. (This is the case in the United States but not in Great Britain. As there is no point system in Britain, it doesn't matter how many dogs are shown in competition. Championship Certificates are awarded at the discretion of the Judge, however few dogs are competing.)

PRE-SHOW PREPARATIONS

As a very basic guide, the following list has been compiled to help you with your preparations for your first point show: the identification ticket sent by the show superintendent, a grooming table, a sturdy tack box in which to carry your dog's grooming tools, a leash to fasten him to the bench or stall and another show lead, your first aid kit, packaged "dog treats," and a supply of food and water for man and beast. Take the largest thermos you can find and a water dish. Remember to feed your dog after the show, not before, and make certain that he exercises and relieves himself before he enters the ring. Many experts think that an exercise pen is mandatory to eliminate the risk of exposing your dog to any diseases in the common exercise ground at shows, but before you bring one along, check the show rules to see if these are allowed. Moreover, exercise pens are useful as places where your dog can

Jane Wiedel of Birch Hill Rottweilers owns this handsome specimen, Ch. Rodsden's Birch Hill Bess, C.D.X., T.D.

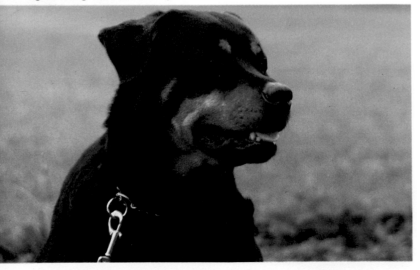

stretch out or rest during your travels or at a motel.

Even take time to think about what you are going to wear on the big day; sports clothes and low-heeled, comfortable shoes are the best. You certainly do not want to wear anything that would distract the judge's attention from your dog; you should merely provide an attractive background for him.

Although your knees may be trembling, try to appear self-confident as you gait (move) and set up the dog. The judging routine usually begins when the judge asks that the dogs be gaited in a circle around the ring while he observes their style, topline, head and tail carriage, reach and drive, and general balance. Avoid going too close to the dog in front of you. Make certain that the judge has an unrestricted view of your dog by keeping him on the inside of the circle, between you and the judge.

Ch. Rodsden's Heiko v Forstwald, C.D., VB, TT, owned by the Michels of Ohio and leased to the McGoverns of New York.

DOG SHOW ETIQUETTE

There are a few "golden rules" to be followed at dog shows which are worth mentioning at this stage. First of all, you are responsible for the behavior of your dog at all times. Keep your dog with you until the showing and keep him under control at all times. Constant vigilance is necessary as thefts have been known at dog shows, as well as poisoning and physical abuse of the animals by jealous exhibitors. You do not want your dog to become involved in a dog fight or taken for a walk by an irresponsible child or one too young to discipline him. In other words, you must not let your dog out of your sight.

Another golden rule is to be punctual; do not be late for your class. Remember that in the ring you must not communicate with the judge or fellow competitors. Watch the judge carefully and follow his instructions. Bear in mind that the ring is not the place to discipline or train your dog; it is too late at this stage! Whatever the judge's decision, accept it with good grace whether you win or lose.

The New Family Member

At long last, the day you have all been waiting for, your new puppy will make its grand entrance into your home. Before you bring your companion to its new residence, however, you must plan carefully for its arrival. Keep in mind that the puppy will need time to adjust to life with a different owner. He may seem a bit apprehensive about the strange surroundings in which he finds himself, having spent the first few weeks of life with his dam and littermates, but in a couple of days, with love and patience on your part, the transition will be complete.

First impressions are important, especially from the puppy's point of view, and these may very well set the pattern of his future relationship with you. You as his keeper and master. Provide him with proper care and attention, and you will be rewarded with a loyal companion for many years. Considering the needs of your puppy and planning ahead will surely make the change from his former home to his new one easier.

ADVANCE PREPARATION

In preparing for your puppy's arrival, perhaps more important than anything else is to find out from the seller how the pup was maintained. What brand of food was offered and when and how often was the puppy fed? Has the pup been housebroken; if so, what method was employed? Attempt to continue whatever routine was started by the person from whom you bought your

Many airlines supply animal carriers for you to purchase; these are necessary if you plan to ship your dog by air.

puppy, then, gradually, you can make those changes that suit you and your lifestyle. If, for example, the puppy has been paper trained, plan to stock up on newspaper. Place this newspaper toilet facility in

must be consistent, always, in the way you handle your pet so that he learns what is expected of him. He must come to trust and respect you a selected spot so that your puppy learns to use the designated area as its "bathroom." And keep on hand a supply of the dog food to which he is accustomed, as check-ups, inoculations, and prompt medical attention in case of illness or an emergency. Find out if the animal you have selected has been vaccinated against

a sudden switch to new food could cause digestive upsets.

Another consideration is sleeping and resting quarters. Be sure to supply a dog bed for your pup, and introduce him to his special cozy corner so that he knows where to retire when he feels like taking a snooze. You'll need to buy a collar (or harness) and leash, a safe chew item (such as Nylabone® or Gumabone®), and a few grooming tools as well. A couple of sturdy feeding dishes, one for food and one for water, will be needed; and it will be necessary, beforehand, to set up a feeding station.

Chain-link fencing is a good, sturdy material to use for building dog runs and kennels.

canine diseases, and make certain you secure all health certificates at the time of purchase. This information will be valuable to your veterinarian, who will want to know the puppy's complete medical history. Incidentally, don't wait until your puppy becomes sick before you seek the services of a vet; make an appointment for your pup before or soon after he takes up residence with you so that he starts out with a clean bill of health in his new home.

FINDING A VETERINARIAN

An important part of your preparations should include finding a local veterinarian who can provide quality health care in the form of routine

CHILDREN AND PUPPIES

Prepare the young members of the household on pet care. Children should learn not only to love their charges but to respect them and treat them with the consideration one would give all living things. It must be emphasized to youngsters that the puppy has certain needs, just as humans have, and all family members must take an active role in ensuring that these needs are met. Someone must feed the puppy. Someone must walk him a couple of times a day or clean up after him if he is trained to relieve himself on newspaper. Someone must groom his coat, clean his ears, and clip his nails from time to time. Someone must see to it that the puppy gets sufficient exercise and squeezing and hugging the animal in ways which are irritating or even painful. Others have been found guilty of teasing, perhaps unintentionally, and disturbing their pet while the animal is eating or resting. One must teach a child, therefore, when and how to gently stroke and fondle a puppy. In time, the child can learn how to carefully pick up and handle the pup. A dog should always be supported with both hands, *not* lifted by the scruff of the neck. One hand placed under the chest, between the front legs, and the other hand supporting the dog's rear end

attention each day.

A child who has a pet to care for learns responsibility; nonetheless, parental guidance is an essential part of his learning experience. Many a child has been known to "love a pet to death,"

Best Brood Bitch at the Canadian National Specialty, l982, was Can. Ch. Trollegens Gundi, here pictured with two of her daughters. Gundi is owned by Marie Kanera, British Columbia, Canada.

will be comfortable and will restrain the animal as you hold and carry him. Always demonstrate to children the proper way to lift a dog.

BE A GOOD NEIGHBOR

For the sake of your dog's safety and well being, don't allow him to wander onto the property of others. Keep him confined at all times to your own yard or indoors where he won't become a nuisance. Consider what dangers lie ahead for an unleashed dog that has total freedom of the great outdoors, particularly when he is unsupervised by his master. There are cars and trucks to dodge on the streets and highways. There are stray animals with which to wrangle. There are poisons all around, such as car antifreeze in driveways or toxic plants and shrubs, which, if swallowed, could prove fatal. There are dognappers and sadistic people who may steal or bring harm to your beloved pet. In short, there are all sorts of nasty things waiting to hurt him. Did you know that if your dog consumes rotting garbage, there is the possibility he could go into shock or even die? And are you aware that a dog left to roam in a wooded area or field could become infected with any number of parasites if he plays with or ingests some small prey, such as a rabbit, that might be carrying these parasitic organisms? A thorn from a rosebush

Am. and Can. Ch. Ivan von Gruenerwald, owned by Forrest Wells, leaps into the air to catch a flying disc. Rottweilers need frequent exercise to keep them mentally and physically sound.

imbedded in the dog's foot pad, tar from a newly paved road stuck to his coat, or a wound inflicted by a wild animal all can be avoided if you take the precaution of keeping your dog in a safe enclosure where he will be protected from such dangers. Don't let your dog run loose; he is likely to stray from home and get into all sorts of trouble.

Many cities and towns now have ordinances that apply to keeping dogs as pets, and in a number of these municipalities there are animal control officials or dog wardens whose job it is to enforce these regulations. In fact, in certain areas there are fines imposed on dog owners who are negligent about controlling their animals. One such familiar regulation involves the curbing of dogs, for sanitary as well as esthetic reasons. In quite a few areas, dog owners are prohibited from allowing their canines, whether leashed or unleashed, to defecate or urinate on someone else's property. There are laws in most places which require dogs to be licensed and inoculated against the dread disease, rabies. Laws, of course, vary from place to place, so save yourself from legal headaches by finding out which rules in your

Housebreaking your dog can be made easier by using a "pooper scooper," a long-handled tool for picking up fecal matter outdoors or inside kennels and runs.

community apply to you as a dog owner. The laws, it should be mentioned, are designed not only to protect the citizenry from acts of canine destruction; they also serve as protection for your dog! So don't wait until your pooch accidentally mauls a young child or scatters the contents of your neighbor's

new environment. Avoid introducing the pup to the family around holiday time, since all of the extra excitement will only add to the confusion and frighten him. Let the puppy enter your home on a day when the routine is normal. For those people who work during the week, a Saturday morning is

Well-constructed dog houses should offer protection from the elements. This model has a "front porch" and the back room serves as the dog's sleeping quarters.

garbage cans or digs holes in carefully cultivated flower beds to exercise your responsibility. Start with a proper attitude as soon as your four-legged companion becomes part of your family.

GETTING ACQUAINTED

Plan to bring your new pet home in the morning so that by nightfall he will have had some time to become acquainted with you and his

an ideal time to bring the puppy to his new home; this way he has the entire weekend to make adjustments before being left alone for a few hours, come Monday morning.

Let the puppy explore, under your watchful eye of course, and let him come to know his new home without stress and fear. Resist the temptation to handle him too much during these first few days. And, if there are other dogs or animals around the house, make certain all are properly introduced. If you observe fighting among the

47

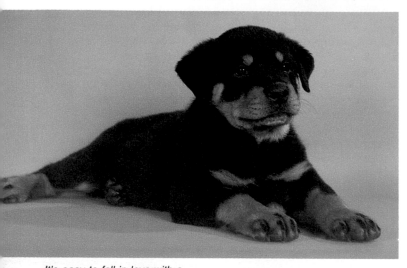

It's easy to fall in love with a Rottie pup, but before you do, make certain this is the breed that suits your lifestyle.

A von Stolzenfels puppy owned by Evelyn Ellman, Michigan.

animals, or some other problem, you may have to separate all parties until they learn to accept one another. Remember that neglecting your other pets while showering the new puppy with extra attention will only cause animosity and jealousy. Make an effort to pay special attention to the other animals as well.

On that eventful first night, try not to give in and let the puppy sleep with you; otherwise, this could become a difficult habit to break. Let him cry and whimper, even if it means a night of restlessness for the entire family. Some people have had success with putting a doll or a hot water bottle wrapped in a towel in the puppy's bed as a surrogate mother, while others have placed a ticking alarm clock in the bed to simulate the heartbeat of the pup's dam and littermates. Remember that this furry little fellow is used to the warmth and security of his mother and siblings, so the adjustment to sleeping alone will take time. Select a location away from drafts and away from the feeding station for placement of his dog bed. Keep in mind, also, that the bed should be roomy enough for him to stretch out in; as he grows older, you may need to supply a larger one.

Prior to the pup's arrival, set up his room and partition it the way you would to keep an infant out of a particular area. You may want to keep his bed, his feeding station, and his toilet area all in the same room—in separate locations—or you may want to set the feeding station up in your kitchen, perhaps, where meals for all family members are served. Whatever you decide, do it ahead of time so that you will have that much less to worry about when your puppy finally moves in with you.

Above all else, be patient with your puppy as he adjusts to life in his new home. If you purchased a pup that is not housebroken, you will have to spend time with the dog—just as you would with a small child—until he develops proper toilet habits. Even a housebroken puppy may feel nervous in strange new surroundings and have an occasional accident. Praise and encouragement will elicit

far better results than punishment or scolding. Remember that your puppy wants nothing more than to please you.

Is this Rottweiler the team mascot for Michigan State?—if not, he ought to be. Kava von Stolzenfels, C.D.X. is owned by Evelyn Ellman of Michigan.

Feeding Requirements

Soon after your puppy comes to live with you, he will need to be fed. As mentioned already, ask the seller what foods were offered the youngster and stay with that diet for a while. It is important for the puppy to keep eating and to avoid skipping a meal, so entice him with the food to which he is accustomed. If you prefer to switch to some other brand of dog food, each day begin to add small quantities of the new brand to

relatively inexpensive to prepare. Puppies need to be fed small portions at frequent intervals, since they are growing and their activity level is high. You must ensure that your pup gains weight steadily; with an adult dog,

Food and water dishes need to be washed with soap and hot water and rinsed well each day. Select ones that are easy to clean and heavy so that they won't tip over.

the usual food offering. Make the portions of the new food progressively larger until the pup is weaned from his former diet.

What should you feed the puppy and how often? His diet is really quite simple and

however, growth slows down and weight must be regulated to prevent obesity and a host of other problems. At one time it was thought that home-cooked meals were the answer, with daily rations of meat, vegetables, egg yolk, cereal, cheese, brewer's yeast, and vitamin supplements. With all of the nutritionally complete commercial dog food products readily available, these time-consuming preparations really are unnecessary now. A great deal of money and research

Sound nutrition is important to good health. A proper diet for your dog—based on his age and condition—helps to ensure strong, healthy bones. The skeletal system of Canis familiaris *is very similar in many ways to that of* Homo sapiens.

has resulted in foods that we can serve our dogs with confidence and pride; and most of these commercial foods have been developed along strict guidelines according to the size, weight, and age of your dog. These products are reasonably priced, easy to find, and convenient to store.

THE PUPPY'S MEALS

After a puppy has been fully weaned from its mother until approximately three months of age, it needs to be fed four times a day. In the morning and evening offer kibble (dog meal) soaked in hot water or broth, to which you have added some canned meat-based food or fresh raw meat cut into small chunks. At noon and bedtime feed him a bit of kibble or whole-grain cereal moistened with milk (moistening, by the way, makes the food easier to digest, since dogs don't typically chew their food). From three to six months, increase the portion size and offer just three meals—one milk and two meat. At six months, two meals are sufficient; at one year, a

(Top) Frohlich von Stolzenfels with pups. (Bottom) Yes, Rottweilers even make good sled dogs! Testimony to that fact is the Green Mountain Sled Team, owned by Anthony Attalla of New Hampshire.

single meal can be given, supplemented with a few dry biscuits in the morning and evening. During the colder months, especially if your dog is active, you might want to mix in some wheat germ oil or corn oil or bacon drippings with the meal to add extra calories. Remember to keep a bowl of cool, fresh water on hand always to help your dog regulate its body temperature and to aid in digestion.

From one year on, you may continue feeding the mature dog a single meal (in the evening, perhaps, when you have your supper), or you may prefer to divide this meal in two, offering half in the morning and the other half at

COMPARISON SHOPPING

With so many fine dog-food products on the market today, there is something for everyone's pet. You may want to serve dry food "as is" or mix it with warm water or broth. Perhaps you'll choose to combine dry food with fresh or canned preparations. Some canned foods contain

Jan Marshall of Vermont owns this impressive trio: Ch. Donnaj Vt. Yankee of Paulus, C.D.X., TT and his two sons, Ch. Donnaj Crusader and Ch. Donnaj Eagle.

night. Keep in mind that while puppies require foods in small chunks, or nuggets, older dogs can handle larger pieces of food at mealtime. Discuss your dog's feeding schedule with your veterinarian; he can make suggestions about the right diet for your particular canine friend.

all meat, but they are not complete; others are mixtures of meat and grains, which have been fortified with additional nutrients to make them complete and balanced. There are also various packaged foods that can be served alone or as supplements and that can be left out for a few hours without spoiling. This self-feeding method, which works well for dogs that are not prone to overweight problems, allows the animal to serve himself whenever he feels hungry. Many people who work during the day find these dry or semi-moist rations convenient to use, and these foods are great to bring along if you travel with your dog.

Be sure to read the labels carefully before you make your dog-food purchases. Most reputable pet-food manufacturers list the ingredients and the nutritional content right on the can or package. Instructions are usually included, besides, so that you will know how much to feed your dog to keep him thriving and in top condition. A varied, well-balanced diet that supplies the proper amounts of protein, carbohydrate, fat, vitamins, minerals, and water is important to keep your puppy healthy and to guarantee its normal development. Adjustments to the diet can

The advantage of heavy, or weighted, food and water dishes is that they won't tip over while your dog is eating or drinking. The size of your dog should determine the size of the bowl you select for him.

be made, under your veterinarian's supervision, according to the individual puppy, his rate of growth, his activity level, and so on. Liquid or powder vitamin and mineral supplements, or those in tablet form, are available and can be given if you need to feel certain that the diet is balanced.

DEVELOPING GOOD EATING HABITS

Try to serve your puppy its meals at the same time each day and in the same location so that he will get used to his daily routine and develop good eating habits. A bit of raw egg, cottage cheese, or table scraps (leftover food from your own meals) can be offered from time to time; but never accustom your dog to eating human "junk food." Cake, candy, chocolate, soda, and other snack foods are for people, not dogs. Besides, these foods provide only "empty" calories that your pet doesn't need if he is to stay healthy. Avoid offering spicy, fried, fatty, or starchy foods, rather, offer leftover meats, vegetables, and gravies. Get in the habit of feeding your puppy or your grown dog his *own* daily meals of dog food. If ever you are in doubt about what foods and how much to serve, consult your veterinarian.

ALL DOGS NEED TO CHEW

Puppies and young dogs need something with

Automatic waterers are convenient to use and provide a constant water supply for your dog.

resistance to chew on while their teeth and jaws are developing—for cutting the puppy teeth, to induce growth of the permanent teeth under the puppy teeth, to assist in getting rid of the puppy teeth at the proper time, to help the permanent teeth through the gums, to assure normal jaw development and to settle the permanent teeth solidly in the jaws.

The adult dog's desire to chew stems from the instinct for tooth cleaning, gum massage and jaw exercise— plus the need to vent periodic doggie tensions.

Dental caries, as it affects the teeth of humans, is virtually unknown in dogs; but tartar accumulates on the teeth of dogs, particularly at the gum line, more rapidly than on the teeth of humans. These accumulations, if not removed, bring irritation and then infection, which erodes the tooth enamel and ultimately destroys the teeth at the roots.

Tooth and jaw development will normally continue until the

(Top) Von Gailingen's Joie De Vivre, by Ks. Ch. Condor zur Klamm, SchH. III, FH ex Am. and Can. Ch. Von Gailingen's Dassie Did It, U.D.T., Can. C.D., owned by Catherine Thompson of New Jersey. (Bottom) Eight-week-old Erdelied Zebest, daughter of top producer Ch. Graudstark's Luger, C.D. ex Ch. Daba von Andan. Bred and owned by Surely Rawlings of Florida.

dog is more than a year old— but sometimes much longer, depending upon the dog, chewing exercise, the rate at which calcium can be utilized and many other factors, known and unknown, which affect the development of individual dogs. Diseases, like distemper for example, may sometimes arrest development of the teeth and jaws, which may resume months or even years later.

This is why dogs, especially puppies and young dogs, will

Gumabone® is the safest chew toy that you can give your dog— it's proven to be safer and lasts at least ten times longer than similar products made of rawhide, rubber, or vinyl. When the Gumabone® wears down, as indicated in this photo, simply replace it with a new one.

often destroy valuable property when their chewing instinct is not diverted from their owner's possessions, particularly during the widely varying critical period for young dogs. Saving your possessions from destruction, assuring proper development of teeth and jaws, providing for "interim" tooth cleaning and gum massage, and channeling doggie tensions into a non-destructive outlet are, therefore, all dependent upon the dog's having something suitable for chewing readily available

when his instinct tells him to chew. If your purposes, and those of your dog, are to be accomplished, what you provide for chewing must be desirable from the doggie viewpoint, have the necessary functional qualities, and, above all, be safe for your dog.

It is very important that dogs not be permitted to chew on anything they can break or indigestible things from which they can bite sizeable chunks. Sharp pieces, such as those from a bone which can be broken by a dog, may pierce the intestine wall and kill. Indigestible things which can be bitten off in chunks, such as toys made of rubber compound or cheap plastic, may cause an intestinal stoppage; if not regurgitated, they are certain to bring painful death unless surgery is promptly performed.

Strong natural bones, such

Nylabone® products come in a variety of shapes, sizes, and flavors to suit every dog's taste. Since these therapeutic devices help cleanse your dog's teeth and massage his gums, they are highly recommended by veterinarians.

as 4 to 8 inch lengths of round shin bone from mature beef—either the kind you can get from your butcher or one of the varieties available commercially in pet stores—may serve your dog's teething needs, if his mouth is large enough to handle them effectively.

You may be tempted to give your puppy a smaller bone and he may not be able to break it when you do, but puppies grow rapidly and the power of their jaws constantly increases until maturity. This means that a growing dog

may break one of the smaller bones at any time, swallow the pieces and die painfully before you realize what is wrong.

Many people have the mistaken notion that their dog's teeth are like those of wild carnivores or of dogs from antiquity. The teeth of wild carnivorous animals and those found in the fossils of the dog-like creatures of antiquity have far thicker and stronger enamel than those of our contemporary dogs.

All hard, natural bones are highly abrasive. If your dog is an avid chewer, natural bones may wear away his teeth prematurely; hence, they then

Dogs love to chase and catch flying discs, and the Nylabone® Corporation has manufactured several types to please every dog and his owner! Nyladisc® is made of flavored, annealed nylon and features a molded bone on top that makes the disc easier for your dog to pick up. Chocolate Nyladisc® is the chocolate version of Nyladisc®. Gumadisc® is made of soft, flavored annealed polyurethane and also has a molded bone on top for easy retrieval by your dog. Pet shops and veterinarians everywhere endorse these products and can tell you more about them.

should be taken away from your dog when the teething purposes have been served. The badly worn, and usually painful, teeth of many mature dogs can be traced to excessive chewing on animal bones. Contrary to popular belief, knuckle bones that can be chewed up and swallowed by the dog provide little, if any, useable calcium or other nutriment. They do, however, disturb the digestion of most dogs and might cause them to vomit the nourishing food they really need.

Never give a dog your old shoe to chew on, even if you have removed all the nails or metal parts, such as lace grommets, buckles, metal arches, and so on. Rubber heels are especially dangerous, as the dog can bite off chunks, swallow them, and suffer from intestinal blockage as a result. Additionally, if the rubber should happen to have a nail imbedded in it that you cannot detect, this could pierce or tear the intestinal wall. There is always the possibility, too, that your dog may fail to differentiate between his shoe and yours and chew up a good pair while you're not looking. It is strongly recommended that you refrain from offering old shoes as chew toys since there are much safer products available.

Rawhide products have become very popular. However they don't serve the primary chewing functions very well, they are a bit messy when wet from mouthing, and most dogs chew them up rather rapidly. They have been considered safe for dogs until recently. Now, more and more incidents of death, and near death, by strangulation have been reported to be the result of partially swallowed chunks of rawhide swelling in the throat. Currently, some veterinarians have been attributing cases of acute constipation to large pieces of incompletely digested rawhide in the intestine.

The nylon bones, especially those with natural meat and bone fractions added, are probably the most complete, safe and economical answer to the chewing need. Dogs cannot break them or bite off sizeable chunks; hence, they are completely safe. And being longer lasting than other things offered for the purpose, they are economical.

Hard chewing raises little bristle-like projections on the surface of the nylon bones to provide effective interim tooth cleaning and vigorous gum massage, much in the same way your tooth brush does it for you. The little projections are raked off and swallowed in the form of thin shavings, but the chemistry of the nylon is such that they break down in the stomach fluids and pass through without effect.

The toughness of the nylon provides the strong chewing resistance needed for important jaw exercise and effective help for the teething functions; however, there is no tooth wear because nylon is non-abrasive. Being inert, nylon does not support the growth of microorganisms; and it can be washed in soap and water, or it can be sterilized by boiling or in an autoclave.

There are a great variety of Nylabone® products available that veterinarians recommend as safe and healthy for your dog or puppy to chew on. These Nylabone® Pooch Pacifiers® can't splinter, chip, or break off in large chunks; instead, they are frizzled by the dog's chewing action, and this creates a toothbrush-like surface that cleanses the teeth and massages the gums. At the same time, these hard-nylon therapeutic devices channel doggie tension and chewing frustation into constructive rather than destructive behavior. Unfortunately, many nylon chew products have been copied. These inferior quality copies are sold in supermarkets and other chain stores. The really good products are sold only through veterinarians, pet shops, grooming salons and places where the sales people really know something about dogs. The good products have the flavor impregnated INTO the bone. This makes the taste last longer. The smell is undetectable to humans. The artificial bones which have a strong odor are poor-quality bones with the odor sprayed on to impress the dog owner (not the dog)! These heavily scented dog toys may impart the odor to your carpets or furniture if an odor-sprayed bone lies there wet from a dog's chewing on it.

If you want a soft, chewy play toy, look for Gumabone® products wherever Nylabone® products are sold. These flexible toys are available in various sizes of bones, balls, knots, and rings (and even a tug toy) designed to provide safe entertainment for you and your dog. These great aids for teaching your canine companion how to retrieve are made of a soft, thermoplastic polymer that lasts at least ten times longer than other rawhide, rubber, or vinyl chew toys, making them very economical. If your dog is able to chew apart a Gumabone® toy, although most dogs cannot, it is probably because you gave him a Gumabone® toy that was too small. Replace it with a larger one and most likely he will not be able to chew it

Taking Reserve Winners from the puppy class at the 1984 Alaska Kennel Club show is Xanadu's Bronson Jos v Altar, by Ch. Altar's Gaiter vom Axel ex Georgian Court Gaylee. Joann Turner, Alaska, owner.

apart. These ham-flavored toys will provide scores of hours of fun for most dogs that like chewing on soft items.

Nothing, however, substitutes for periodic professional attention to your dog's teeth and gums, not any more than your toothbrush can do that for you. Have your dog's teeth cleaned by your

With the addition of Gumabone® to the arsenal of dog chew toys, petshops are now offering better quality chew toys. It is of the utmost importance that the size of the Gumabone® match the size of the dog. A large dog can chew through, or swallow, a toy too small for it. The great advantage of Nylabone® and Gumabone® is that they are made by a company who ONLY makes dog toys and therapeutic devices. They usually guarantee that their products will last much longer than any chain store or supermarket copy and they will replace the Gumabone® with a larger size, free of charge, if your dog chews it up very quickly. It is normal for a dog to chew on the knuckle. The bone shown above is ready to be replaced, since the knuckle has been chewed down on one end. The small particles of Nylabone® and Gumabone® that the dog chews off normally pass through the digestive tract as roughage.

veterinarian at least once a year—twice a year is better— and he will be healthier, happier and a far more pleasant companion.

FEEDING GUIDELINES

Some things to bear in mind with regard to your dog's feeding regimen follow:

• Nutritional balance, provided by many commercial dog foods, is vital; avoid feeding a one-sided diet of all-meat. Variety in the kinds of meat (beef, lamb, chicken, liver) or cereal grains (wheat, oats, corn) that you offer your dog is of secondary importance compared to the balance or "completeness" of dietary components.

• Always refrigerate opened canned food so that it doesn't

Chocolate-flavored and ham-scented Nylabones® are real favorites with dogs. Incidentally, in the former the thin film of chocolate is just beneath the surface where it can't be washed off or licked off.

spoil. Remember to remove all uneaten portions of canned or moistened food from the feeding dish as soon as the pup has finished his meal. Discard the leftover food immediately and thoroughly wash and dry the

Bred by Dennis and Margaret Teague of California, Kavick vom Chutzpah is owned by Jean Benkowski of Wisconsin.

should be made available at all times, incidentally, even if dry foods are not left out for self-feeding. Each day the water dish should be washed in soap and hot water, rinsed well, and dried; a refill of clean, fresh water should be provided daily.

● Food and water should be served at room temperature, neither too hot nor too cold, so that it is more palatable for your puppy.

● Serve your pup's meals in sturdy hard-plastic, stainless steel, or earthenware containers, ones that won't tip over as the dog bolts his food down. Some bowls and dishes are weighted to prevent spillage, while others fit neatly into holders which offer support. Feeding dishes should be large enough to hold each meal.

● Whenever the nutritional needs of your dog change, that is to say, when it grows old; if it becomes ill, obese, or pregnant; or if it starts to nurse its young, special diets are in order. Always contact your vet for advice on these special dietary requirements.

● Feed your puppy at the same regular intervals each day; reserve treats for special occasions or, perhaps, to reward good behavior during training sessions.

feeding dish, as dirty dishes are a breeding ground for harmful germs.

● When offering dry foods, always keep a supply of water on hand for your dog. Water

Puppies newly weaned from their mother and siblings should be kept warm at all times. As they get older, gradually they can be acclimated to cooler temperatures. When you purchase your dog, find out from the seller whether he is hardy and can withstand the rigors of outdoor living. Many breeds have been known to adapt well to a surprising number of environments, so long as they are given time to adjust. If your pup is to be an indoor companion, perhaps a dog bed in the corner of the family room will suffice, or maybe you'll want to invest in a crate for him to call his "home" whenever he needs to be confined for short intervals. You might plan to partition off a special room, or part of a room, for your pooch; or you may find that a heated garage or finished basement works well as your dog's living quarters. If your

Never allow your dog to ride in the car unconfined; always place him in a crate to ensure his safety.

breed can tolerate living outside, you may want to buy or build him his own dog house with an attached run. Or it might be feasible to place his house in your fenced-in backyard. The breed that can live outdoors fares well when he has access to some sort of warm, dry shelter during periods of inclement weather. As you begin thinking about where your canine friend will spend most of his time, you'll want to consider his breed, his age, his temperament, his need for exercise, and the money, space, and resources you have available to house him.

THE DOG BED

In preparing for your puppy's arrival, it is recommended that a dog bed be waiting for him so that he has a place to sleep and rest. If indeed you have provided him with his own bed or

Portable exercise pens are useful whenever you travel with your dog.

basket, ensure that it is in a warm, dry, draft-free spot that is private but at the same time near the center of family activity. Refrain from placing his bed near the feed and water dishes or his toilet area. You may want to give your puppy something with which to snuggle, such as a laundered towel or blanket or an article of old clothing. Some dogs have been known to chew apart their beds and

Every dog should have a bed of its own. Check your local pet shop for dog beds and other products that you will need to keep your dog healthy and happy.

roomy, comfortable, and easy to clean, keeping in mind that you may have to replace the smaller bed with a larger one as the puppy grows to adulthood. Remember to clean and disinfect the bed and sleeping area from time to time, as these can become parasitic playgrounds for fleas, lice, mites and the like.

THE CRATE

Although many dog lovers may cringe at the mere mention of the word *crate*, thinking of it as a cage or a cruel means of confinement, this handy piece of equipment can be put to good use for puppies and grown dogs alike. Even though you may love your dog to an extraordinary degree, you may not want him to have free rein of the house, particularly when you are not home to supervise him. If used properly, a crate can restrict your dog when it is not

bedding, but you can easily channel this chewing energy into more constructive behavior simply by supplying him with some safe toys or a Nylabone® pacifier for gnawing. Pet shops stock dog beds, among other supplies that you might need for your pup; so select one that is

An alternative to dog beds are baskets, and these are available in various shapes and sizes.

convenient to have him underfoot, *i.e.,* when guests are visiting or during your mealtimes.

A surprising number of dog owners who, originally, had negative feelings about crating their dogs, have had great success using them. The crate itself serves as a bed, provided it is furnished with bedding material, or it can be used as an indoor dog house. Not all dogs readily accept crates or to being confined in them for short intervals, so for them another means of restriction must be found. But for those dogs that do adjust to spending time in these structures, the crate can be useful in many ways. The animal can be confined for a few hours while you are away from home or at work, or you can bring your crated dog along with you in the car when you travel or go on vacation. They also prove handy as carriers whenever you have to transport a sick dog to the veterinarian.

Most crates are made of sturdy wire or plastic and some of the collapsible models can be stored conveniently or folded so that they can be moved easily from room to room or from inside the house to the yard on a warm, sunny day. If you allow your puppy or grown dog to become acquainted with its crate by cleverly propping the door open and leaving some of his favorite toys inside, in no time he will come to regard the crate as his own doggie haven. As with a dog bed, place the crate away from drafts in a dry, warm spot; refrain from placing food and water dishes in it, as these only crowd the space and offer opportunity for spillage.

If you need to confine your puppy so that he can't get into mischief while you're not home, remember to consider the animal's needs at all times. Therefore, select a large crate, one in which the dog can stand up and move around comfortably; in fact, bigger is better in this context. Never leave the animal confined for more than a few hours at a time without letting him out to exercise, play, and, if necessary, relieve himself. Never crate a dog for ten hours, for example, unless you keep the door to the crate open so that he can get out for food and water and to stretch a bit. If long intervals of confinement are necessary, consider placing the unlatched crate in a partitioned section of your house or apartment.

Crates have become the answer for many a dog owner faced with the dilemma of either getting rid of a destructive dog or living with him despite his bad habits. These people who have neither the time nor the patience to train their dogs, or to modify undesirable behavior patterns, can at least restrain their pets during those times they can't be there to supervise. So long as the crate is used in a humane fashion, whereby a dog is confined for no more than a few hours at any one time, it can figure importantly in a dog owner's life. Show dogs, incidentally, learn at an early age that much time will be spent in and out of crates while they are on the show circuit. Many canine celebrities are kept in their crates until they are called to ringside, and they spend many hours crated to and from the shows.

THE DOG HOUSE

These structures, often made of wood, should be made sturdily and offer enough room for your dog to

There is no need to build your dog his own house when there are commercially-made ones from which to choose.

stretch out in when it rests or sleeps. Dog houses that are elevated or situated on a platform protect the animal from cold and dampness that may seep through the ground. Of the breeds that are temperature hardy and will live outdoors, some are housed outside during the daytime only; others are permanent outdoor residents day and night, all year 'round.

If your intention is to have a companion that lives out-of-doors, it will be necessary to provide him with a more elaborate house, one that really protects from him the elements. Make sure the dog's house is constructed of waterproof materials. Furnish him with sufficient bedding to burrow into on a chilly night and provide extra insulation to keep out drafts and wet weather. Add a partition (a kind of room divider which separates the entry area from the main sleeping space) inside his house or attach a swinging door to the entrance to help keep him warm when he is inside his residence. The swinging door facilitates entry to and from the dog house, while at the same time it provides protection, particularly from wind and drafts.

This traditional style dog house is made of non-toxic polymer, which keeps your dog cool in summer and warm in winter; additionally, it is strong, durable, and easy to clean.

Some fortunate owners whose yards are enclosed by high fencing allow their dogs complete freedom within the boundaries of their property. In these situations, a dog can leave its dog house and get all the exercise it wants. Of course such a large space requires more effort to keep clean. An alternative to complete backyard freedom is a dog kennel or run which attaches to or surrounds the dog's house. This restricts some forms of movement, such as running, perhaps, but it does provide ample room for walking, climbing, jumping, and stretching. Another option is to fence off part of the yard and place the dog house in the enclosure. If you need to tether your dog to its house, make certain to use a fairly long lead so as not to hamper the animal's need to move and exercise his limbs.

CLEANLINESS

No matter where your dog lives, either in or out of your home, be sure to keep him in surroundings as clean and sanitary as possible. His excrement should be removed and disposed of every day without fail. No dog should be forced to lie in his own feces. If your dog lives in his own house, the floor should be

The dome-like dog bed— a real doggie haven —features a soft, furry cushion for your dog's comfort.

swept occasionally and the bedding should be changed regularly if it becomes soiled. Food and water dishes need to be scrubbed with hot water and detergent and rinsed well to remove all traces of soap.

The water dish should be refilled with a supply of fresh water. The dog and his environment must be kept free of parasites (especially fleas and mosquitoes, which can carry disease) with products designed to keep these pests under control. Dog crates need frequent scrubbing, too, as do the floors of kennels and runs. Your pet must be kept clean and comfortable at all times; if you exercise strict sanitary control, you will keep disease and parasite infestation to a minimum.

EXERCISE

A well-balanced diet and regular medical attention from a qualified veterinarian are essential in promoting good health for your dog, but so is daily exercise to keep him fit and mentally alert. Dogs that have been confined all day while their owners are at work or school need special attention. There should be some time set aside each day for play—a romp with a family member, perhaps. Not everyone is lucky enough to let his dog run through an open meadow or along a sandy beach, but even a ten-minute walk in the fresh air will do. Dogs that are house-bound, particularly those that live in apartments, need to be walked out-of-doors after each meal so that they can relieve themselves. Owners can make this daily ritual more pleasant both for themselves and their canine companions by combining the walk with a little "roughhousing," that is to say, a bit of fun and togetherness.

Whenever possible, take a stoll to an empty lot, a playground, or a nearby park. Attach a long lead to your dog's collar, and let him run and jump and tone his body through cardiovascular activity. This will help him burn calories and keep him trim, but it will also help relieve tension and stress that may have had a chance to manifest itself while you were away all day. For people who work Monday through Friday, weekend jaunts can be especially beneficial, since there will be more time to spend with your canine friend. You might want to engage him in a simple game of fetch with a stick or a rubber ball. Even such basic tricks as rolling over, standing on the hindlegs, or jumping up (all of which can be done inside the home as well) can provide additional exercise. But if you plan to challenge your dog with a real workout to raise his heart rate, remember not to push him too hard without first warming up with a brisk walk. Don't forget to "cool him down" afterwards with a

Your dog needs regular exercise, and one way to provide this is to toss a flying disc to him a number of times so that he gets a good workout.

rhythmic trot until his heart rate returns to normal. Some dog owners jog with their dogs or take them along on bicycle excursions.

The skeleton of Canis familiaris is similar to that of most mammals, including man.

Housebreaking Your Puppy

The new addition to your family may already have received some basic house training before his arrival in your home. If he has not, remember that a puppy will want to relieve himself about half a dozen times a day; it is up to you to specify where and when he should "do his business." Housebreaking is your first training concern and should begin the moment you bring the puppy home.

There are all sorts of brushes made for grooming dogs; ask your local pet shop for the one that will keep your dog's coat looking its best.

Ideally, puppies should be taken outdoors after meals, as a full stomach will exert pressure on the bladder and colon. What goes into the dog must eventually come out; the period after his meal is the most natural and appropriate time. When he eliminates, he should be praised and this will increase the likelihood of the same thing happening after every meal. He should also be encouraged to use the same area and will probably be attracted to it after frequent use.

OUTDOOR TRAINING

Some veterinarians have maintained that a puppy could learn to urinate and defecate on command if properly trained. The advantage of this conditioning technique is that your pet would associate the act of elimination with a particular word of your invention rather than with a particular time or place which might not always be convenient or available. So whether you were visiting an unfamiliar place or didn't want to go outside with your dog in sub-zero temperatures, he would still be able to relieve himself when he heard the specific command word. Elimination would occur after this "trigger" phrase or word had set up a conditioned reflex in the dog who would eliminate anything contained in his bladder or bowel upon hearing it. The shorter the word, the more you could repeat it and imprint it on your dog's memory.

Your chosen command word should be given simultaneously with the sphincter opening events in order to achieve perfect and rapid conditioning. This is why it is important initially to familiarize yourself with the tell-tale signs preceding your puppy's elimination process. Then you will be prepared to say the word at the crucial moment. There is usually a sense of urgency on the dog's part; he may follow a sniffing and circling pattern which you will soon recognize. It is important to use the command in his usual area only when you know the puppy can eliminate, *i.e.*, when his stomach or bladder is full. He will soon learn to associate the act with the word. One word of advice, however, if you plan to try out this method: never use the puppy's name or any other word which he might frequently hear about the house—you can imagine the result!

Finally, remember that any training takes time. Such a conditioned response can be obtained with intensive practice with any normal, healthy dog over six weeks of age. Even Pavlov's salivating dogs required fifty repetitions before the desired response was achieved. Patience and

cover the specific area where your dog should relieve himself. These should be placed some distance away from his sleeping and feeding area, as a puppy will not urinate or defecate where he eats. When the newspapers are changed, the bottom papers should be placed on top of the new ones in order to evoke the purpose of the papers by scent as well as by sight. He should be praised during or immediately after he has made use of this particular part of the room. Each positive reinforcement increases the possibility of his using that area again.

When he arrives, it is advisable to limit the puppy to

The so-called "pooper scooper" is handy for picking up after your dog. It is especially useful in areas that require you to curb your dog.

persistence will eventually produce results—do not lose heart!

INDOOR TRAINING

Indoors, sheets of newspapers could be used to

one room, usually the kitchen, as it most likely has a linoleum or easily washable floor surface. Given the run of the house, the sheer size of the place will seem overwhelming and confusing and he might leave his "signature" on your furniture or clothes! There will be time later to familiarize him gradually with his new surroundings.

PATIENCE, PERSISTENCE, AND PRAISE

As with a human baby, you must be patient, tolerant, and understanding of your pet's mistakes, making him feel loved and wanted, not rejected and isolated. You wouldn't hit a baby for soiling his diapers as you would realize that he was not yet able to control his bowel movements; be as compassionate with your canine infant. Never rub his nose in his excreta. Never indulge in the common practice of punishing him with a rolled-up newspaper. Never hit a puppy with your hand. He will only become "hand-shy" and learn to fear you. Usually the punishment is meted out sometime after the offense so it loses its efficacy anyway as the bewildered dog cannot connect the two events. Moreover, by association, he will soon learn to be afraid of you and anything to do with newspapers—including, perhaps, that area where he is *supposed* to relieve himself!

Most puppies are eager to please; praise, encourgement, and reward (particularly the food variety) will produce far better results than any scolding or physical punishment. Moreover, it is far better to dissuade your puppy from doing certain things, like chewing on chair legs or other furniture, by making those objects particularly distasteful to him. You could smear them with a generous amount of hot chili sauce or cayenne pepper mixed with petroleum jelly, for example. This would make it

Plan to stock up on newspaper for housebreaking your puppy.

seem as if the object itself was administering the punishment whenever he attempted to chew it. He probably wouldn't need a second reminder!

Remember that the reason a dog has housebreaking or behavior problems is because his owner has allowed them to develop. This is why you must begin as you intend to continue, by letting your dog know what is acceptable and unacceptable behavior. It is also important that you be consistent in your demands; you cannot feed him from the dining room table one day and then punish him when he begs for food from your dinner guests.

TRAINING IS NECESSARY

You will want the newest member of your family to be welcomed by everyone; this will not happen if he urinates in every room of the house or barks all night! He needs training in the correct forms of behavior in this new, human world and you cannot expect your puppy to become the perfect pet overnight. He needs your help in his socialization process. Training greatly facilitates and enhances the relationship of the dog to his owner and to the rest of society. A successfully trained dog can be taken anywhere and behave well with anyone. Indeed, it is that one crucial word—*training*—which can transform an aggressive animal into a peaceful, well-behaved pet. Now, how does this "transformation" take place?

WHEN AND HOW TO TRAIN

Like housebreaking, training should begin as soon as the puppy enters the house. The formal training sessions should be short but frequent, for example, ten to fifteen minute periods three times a day. These are much more effective than long, tiring sessions of half an hour which might soon become boring.

THE COLLAR AND LEASH

Your puppy should become used to a collar and leash as soon as possible. If he is very young, a thin, choke-chain collar could be used, but you will need a larger and heavier one for training when he is a little older. Remember to have his name and address on an identification tag attached to his collar, as you don't want to lose your pet if he should happen to leave your premises and explore the neighborhood!

Let the puppy wear his collar until he is used to how it feels. After a short time he will soon become accustomed to it and you can attach the leash. He might resist your

Some dog owners prefer to use the figure-eight–style harness instead of a collar.

You are building your relationship with your puppy during these times so make them as enjoyable as possible. It is a good idea to have these sessions *before* the puppy's meal, not after it when he wouldn't feel like exerting himself; the dog will then associate something pleasurable with his training sessions and look forward to them.

attempts to lead him or simply sit down and refuse to budge. Fight him for a few minutes, tugging on the leash if necessary, then let him relax for the day. He won't be trained until he learns that he must obey the pull under any circumstance, but this will take a few sessions. Remember that a dog's period of concentration is short, so little and often is the

Nylon-web dog collars have become quite popular and they can be found in a variety of attractive colors.

wisest course of action—and patience is the password to success.

GIVING COMMANDS

When you begin giving your puppy simple commands, make them as short as possible and use the same word with the same meaning at all times, for example, "Heel," "Sit," and "Stay." You must be consistent; otherwise your puppy will become confused. The dog's name should prefix all commands to attract his attention. Do not become impatient with him however many times you have to repeat your command.

A good way to introduce the "Come" command is by calling the puppy when his meal is ready. Once this has been learned, you could call your pet to you at will, always remembering to praise him for his prompt obedience. This "reward" or positive reinforcement is such a crucial part of training that a Director of the New York Academy of Dog Training constructed his whole

A six-foot training lead is a valuable piece of equipment to have on hand when you begin to train your dog.

teaching program upon the methods of "Love, Praise and Reward." Incidentally, if you use the command "Come," use it every time. Don't switch to "Come here" or "Come boy," as this will only confuse your dog.

exercise before his meal. After about five minutes, call him to you, praise him when he arrives, and slip his collar on him. Hold the leash tightly in your right hand; this should force the dog's head up and focus his attention on you. As

If you plan to enter your dog in obedience competition, one exercise he will have to master is the retrieving of a dumbbell.

It is worth underlining the fact that punishment is an ineffective teaching technique. We have already seen this in housebreaking and, for example, if your pup should run away, it would be senseless to beat him when he eventually returns. He would only connect the punishment with his return, not with the running away! Also, never call him to you to punish him, as he will soon learn not to respond when you call his name.

SOME SPECIFIC COMMANDS

"Sit." This is one of the easiest and most useful commands for your dog to learn, so it is a good idea to begin with it. The only equipment required is a leash, collar, and a few tasty tidbits. Take your dog out for some

you say "Sit" in a loud, clear voice, with your left hand press steadily on his rump until he is in a sitting position. As soon as he is in the correct position, praise him and give him the tidbit you have in your hand. Now wait a few minutes to let him rest and repeat the routine. Through repetition, the dog soon associates the word with the act. Never make the lesson too long. Eventually your praise will be reward enough for your puppy.

"Sit-Stay/Stay." To teach your pet to remain in one place or "stay" on your command, first of all order him to the sitting position at your side. Lower your left hand with the flat of your palm in front of his nose and your fingers pointing downwards. Hold the leash high and taut behind his head so that he cannot move. Speak the command "Sit-stay" and, as you are giving it, step in front of him. Repeat the command and tighten the leash so the animal cannot follow you. Walk completely around him, repeating the command and keeping him motionless by holding the leash at arm's length above him to check his

nylon cord or rope about twenty to thirty feet long. Repeat the whole routine from the beginning and be ready to prevent any movement towards you with a sharp "Sit-stay." Move around him in ever-widening circles until you are about fifteen feet away from him. If he still remains seated, you can pat yourself on the back! One useful thing

Another activity at obedience trials involves the dog's retrieving and leaping over the high jump.

movement. When he remains in this position for about fifteen seconds, you can begin the second part of the training. You will have to exchange the leash for a

to remember is that the dog makes associations with what you say, how you say it, and what you do while you are saying it. Do give this command in a firm, clear tone of voice, perhaps using an admonishing forefinger raised in warning to the dog to "stay."

TEACHING TO "HEEL," "COME" AND "DOWN"

When you walk your dog, you should hold the leash firmly in your right hand. The dog should walk on your left so you have the leash crossing your body. This enables you to have greater control over the dog.

Let your dog lead you for the first few moments so that he fully understands that freedom can be his if he goes about it properly. He knows already that when he wants to go outdoors the leash and collar are necessary, so he has respect for the leash. Now, if while walking he starts to pull in one direction, all you do is *stop walking.* He will walk a few steps and then find that he can't walk any further. He will then turn and look into your face. *This is the crucial point!* Just stand there for a moment and stare right back at him . . . now walk another ten feet and stop again. Again your dog will probably walk out the leash, find he can't go any further, and turn around and look again. If he starts to pull and jerk, then just stand there. After he quiets down, just bend down and comfort him as he may be frightened. Keep up this training until he learns not to outwalk you.

"Heel." Once the puppy obeys the pull of the leash,

This is the correct way to place a choke chain on your dog. When placed correctly around the dog's neck, the chain should slacken when there is no pressure exerted from the lead attached to the collar.

half of your training is accomplished. "Heeling" is a necessity for a well-behaved dog, so teach him to walk beside you, head even with your knee. Nothing looks sadder than a big dog taking his helpless owner for a walk. It is annoying to passers-by and other dog owners to have a large dog, however friendly, bear down on them and entangle dogs, people, and packages.

To teach your dog, start off walking briskly, saying "Heel" in a firm voice. Pull back with a sharp jerk if he lunges ahead, and if he lags repeat the command and tug on the leash, not allowing him to drag behind. After the dog has learned to heel at various speeds on leash, you can remove it and practice heeling free, but have it ready to snap on again as soon as he wanders.

"Come." Your dog has already learned to come to you when you call his name. Why? Because you only call him when his food is ready or when you wish to play with him or praise him. Outdoors such a response is more difficult to achieve as he is happily playing by himself or with other dogs. So he must

81

be trained to come to you when he is called. To teach him to come, let him reach the end of a long lead, then give the command, gently pulling him towards you at the same time. As soon as he associates the word *come* with the action of moving toward you, pull only when he does not respond

immediately. As he starts to come, move back to make him learn that he must come from a distance as well as when he is close to you. Soon you may be able to practice without a leash, but if he is slow to come or actively disobedient, go to him and pull him toward you, repeating the command. Always remember to reward his successful completion of a task.

"Down." A puppy is naturally affectionate and excitable. However, not everyone likes to have a playful pup pounce on them with muddy paws or enthusiastically jump up to greet them. It is important that your puppy understands the command, "Down," and it should be one of the first lessons you teach.

One successful teaching strategy is to raise your knee and bump the dog in the stomach as he jumps up; you use this maneuver when puppies rush at you and leap at your chest. Or you could take him by his front legs and move him backward across the floor until he loses his balance and falls over. It will take patience and persistence before he gets the message but you will avoid a lot of dirty clothes and irate neighbors if you persevere!

With this Gumabone® tug toy, manufactured by the Nylabone Corporation, you and your canine companion can get some real exercise!

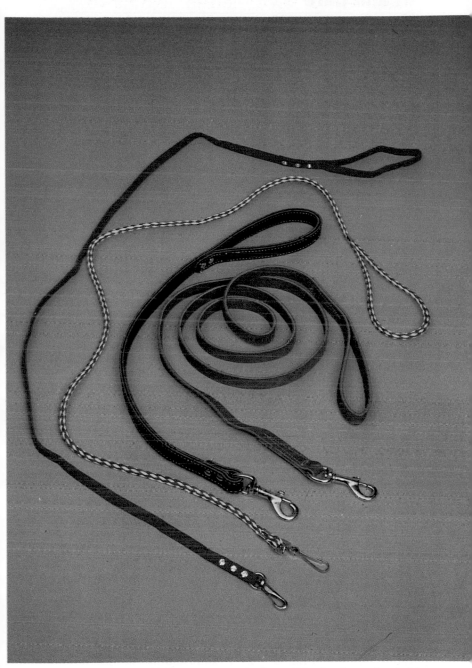

Leads come in a wide assortment of colors, widths, lengths, and materials. What is most important is that the lead you use be strong enough to hold the weight of your dog.

From the moment you purchase your puppy, the most important person in both your lives becomes your veterinarian. His professional advice and treatment will ensure the good health of your pet and he is the first person to call when illness or accidents occur. Do *not* try to be your own veterinarian or apply human remedies to canine diseases.

However, just as you would keep a first aid kit handy for minor injuries sustained by members of your family at home, so you should keep a similar kit prepared for your pet. First aid for your dog would consist of stopping any bleeding, cleaning the wound, and preventing infection. Thus your kit might contain medicated powder, gauze bandages, and adhesive tape to be used in case of cuts. If the cut is deep and bleeding profusely, the bandage should be applied very tightly to help in the formation of a clot. A tight bandage should not be kept in place longer than necessary, so take your pet to the veterinarian immediately.

Walking or running on a cut pad prevents the cut from healing. Proper suturing of the cut and regular changing of the bandages should have your pet's wound healed in a week to ten days. A minor cut should be covered with a light bandage, for you want as much air as possible to reach the wound. Do not apply wads of cotton to a wound as they

will stick to the area and may cause contamination.

You should also keep some hydrogen peroxide available as it is useful in cleaning wounds and is also one of the best and simplest emetics known. Cotton applicator swabs are useful for applying ointment or removing debris from the eyes. A pair of tweezers

When treating an abscess, your veterinarian will begin by twisting some cotton or a cotton ball over the end of a round stick. He then will dip the cotton in an antiseptic solution and set it aside.

should also be kept handy for removing foreign bodies from the dog's throat or body.

Nearly everything a dog might contract in the way of sickness has basically the same set of symptoms: loss of appetite, diarrhea, dull eyes, dull coat, warm and/or runny nose, and a high temperature. Therefore, it is most important to take his temperature at the first sign of illness. To do this, you will need a rectal thermometer which should be lubricated

The vet cuts through the skin covering the abscess (top) with a sterilized sharp knife or razor blade and (right) gently squeezes out the pus, removing it with cotton.

with petroleum jelly. Carefully insert it into the rectum, holding it in place for at least two minutes. It must be held firmly; otherwise there is the danger of its being sucked up into the rectum, or slipping out, thus giving an inaccurate reading. The normal temperature for a dog is between 101° and 102.5°F. If your pet is seriously ill or injured in an accident, your veterinarian will advise you what to do before he arrives.

IF YOUR PET SWALLOWS POISON

A poisoned dog must be treated instantly; any delay could cause his death. Different poisons act in different ways and require different treatments. If you know the dog has swallowed an acid, alkali, gasoline, or kerosene, do not induce vomiting. Give milk to dilute the poison and rush him to the vet. If you can find the

He inserts the cotton, which is at the end of the stick, into the wound. Next he cuts off this cotton plug, as shown, and holds it in place with a piece of adhesive tape to let the wound heal from the inside out.

bottle or container of poison, check the label to see if there is a recommended antidote. If not, try to induce vomiting by giving him a mixture of hydrogen peroxide and water. Mix the regular drugstore strength of hydrogen peroxide (3%) with an equal part of water but do not attempt to pour it down your dog's throat as that could cause inhalation pneumonia. Instead, simply pull the dog's lips away from the side of his mouth, making a pocket for depositing the liquid. Use at least a tablespoonful of the mixture for every ten pounds of your dog's weight. He will vomit in about two minutes. When his stomach has settled, give him

a teaspoonful of Epsom salts in a little water to empty the intestine quickly. The hydrogen peroxide, on ingestion, becomes oxygen and water and is harmless to your dog, but it is the best antidote for phosphorus, which is often used in rat poisons. After you have administered this emergency treatment to your pet and his stomach and bowels have been emptied, rush him to your veterinarian for further care.

DANGER IN THE HOME

There are numerous household products that can prove fatal if ingested by your pet. These include rat poison,

Bone fractures. 1—simple (bones don't penetrate skin); 2—comminuted (small fragments); 3—compound (bone protrudes through skin); 4—greenstick; 5—broken ball of femur.

antifreeze, boric acid, hand soap, detergents, insecticides, mothballs, household cleansers, bleaches, de-icers, polishes and disinfectants, paints and varnish removers, acetone, turpentine, and even health and beauty aids if ingested in large enough quantities. A word to the wise should be sufficient: what you would keep locked away from your two-year-old child, also keep hidden from your pet.

There is another area where danger lurks within the home and that is among the household plants, which are almost all poisonous, even if swallowed in small quantities. There are hundreds of poisonous plants in the United States, among which are: ivy leaves, cyclamen, lily of the valley, rhododendrons, tulip bulbs, azalea, wisteria, poinsettia leaves, mistletoe, daffodils, delphiniums, foxglove leaves, the jimson weed—we cannot name them all. Rhubarb leaves, for example, either raw or cooked, can cause death or violent convulsions. Peach, elderberry, and cherry trees can cause cyanide poisoning if their bark is consumed.

There are also many insects poisonous to dogs such as cockroaches, spiders, flies, and butterflies. Toads and frogs exude a fluid that can make a dog foam at the mouth—and even kill him—if he bites too hard!

There have been cases of dogs suffering nicotine poisoning by consuming the contents of full ashtrays which thoughtless smokers have left on the coffee table. Also, do not leave nails, staples, pins, or other sharp objects lying around and don't let your puppy play with plastic bags which could suffocate him. Unplug, remove, or cover any electrical cords or wires near your dog. Chewing live wires could lead to severe mouth burns or death. Remember that an ounce of prevention is

87

worth a pound of cure: keep all potentially dangerous objects out of your pet's reach.

PROTECT YOURSELF FIRST

In almost all first aid situations, the dog is in pain. He may also be in shock and not appear to be suffering, that is until you move him. Then he may bite your hand or resist being helped at all. So if you want to help your dog, help yourself first by tying his mouth closed. To do this, use a piece of strong cloth four inches wide and three feet long, depending on the size of the dog. Make a loop in the middle of the strip and slip it over his nose with the knot under his chin and over the bony part of his nose. Pull it tight and bring the ends back around his head behind the ears and tie it tightly, ending with a bow knot for quick, easy release. Now you can handle the dog safely. As a dog perspires through his tongue, do not leave the "emergency muzzle" on any longer than necessary.

ADMINISTERING MEDICINE

When you are giving liquid medicine to your dog, it is a good idea to pull the lips away from the side of the mouth, form a lip pocket, and let the liquid trickle past the tongue. Remain at his side, never in front of the dog, as he may cough and spray you with the liquid. Moreover, you must never pour liquid medicine

directly on the tongue as inhalation pneumonia could be the disastrous result.

Medicine in pill form is best administered by forcing the dog's mouth open, holding his head back, and placing the capsule as far back on his tongue as you can reach. Put the palm of your hand over the dog's muzzle (his foreface) with your fingers on one side of his jaw, your thumb on the other. Press his lips hard against his teeth while using your other hand to pull down his lower jaw. With your two fingers, try to put the pill as far back on the dog's tongue as you can reach. Keep his mouth and nostrils closed and he should be

Posterior view of the eye with the lens sectioned. Eye care is important in dogs, so have your veterinarian examine your dog periodically.

forced to swallow the medicine. As the dog will not be feeling well, stroke his neck to comfort him and to help him swallow his medicine more easily. Do keep an eye on him for a few moments

If you see your dog "scooting" on its rear end or rubbing and licking its anus, the animal may have impacted anal glands. Your veterinarian will express the anal glands by first lifting the dog's tail. Next, he places his thumb and index finger on either side of the anus. He squeezes gently until the material is exuded and collects this in a paper towel or cotton gauze. The process may have to be repeated a few times.

afterward, however, to make certain that he does not spit it out.

IN CASE OF AN ACCIDENT

It is often difficult for you to assess the dog's injuries after a road accident. He may appear normal but there might be internal hemorraging. A vital organ could be damaged or ribs broken. Keep the dog as quiet and warm as possible; cover him with blankets or your coat to let his own body heat build up. Signs of shock are a rapid and weak pulse, glassy-eyed appearance, subnormal temperature, and slow capillary refill time. To determine the last symptom, press firmly against the dog's gums until they turn white. Release and count the number of seconds until the gums return to their normal color. If it is more than 2-3 seconds, the dog may be going into shock. Failure to return to the reddish pink color indicates the dog may be in serious trouble and needs immediate assistance.

If artificial respiration is required, first open the dog's mouth and check for obstructions; extend his tongue and examine the pharynx. Clear his mouth of mucus and blood and hold the mouth slightly open. Mouth-to-mouth resuscitation involves holding the dog's tongue to the bottom of his mouth with one hand and sealing his nostrils with the other while you blow into his

To take your dog's pulse, rest one of your fingers on the femoral artery which runs down the inner surface of his hind leg.

mouth. Watch for his chest to rise with each inflation. Repeat every 5-6 seconds or 10-12 breaths a minute.

If the veterinarian cannot come to you try to improvise a stretcher to take the dog to him. To carry a puppy, wrap him in a blanket that has been folded into several thicknesses. If he is in shock, it is better to pick him up by holding one hand under his chest, the other under the hindquarters. This will keep him stretched out.

It is always better to roll an injured dog than to try and lift him. Suppose you find him lying beside the road after a car accident. Apply a muzzle even if you have to use someone's necktie to make one. Send someone for a blanket and roll him gently onto it. Two people, one on each side, can make a stretcher out of the blanket and move the dog easily.

If no blanket is available and the injured dog must be moved, try to keep him as flat as possible. So many dogs' backs are broken in car accidents that one must first consider that possibility. However, if he can move his hind legs or tail, his spine is probably not broken. Get medical assistance for him immediately.

It should be mentioned that unfortunate car accidents, which can maim or kill your dog, can be avoided if he is confined at all times either indoors or, if out-of-doors, in a fenced-in yard or some other protective enclosure. *Never* allow your dog to roam free; even a well-trained dog may, for some unknown reason, dart into the street . . . and the result could be tragic.

If you need to walk your dog, leash him first so that he will be protected from moving vehicles.

PROTECTING YOUR PET

It is important to watch for any tell-tale signs of illness so that you can spare your pet any unnecessary suffering. Your dog's eyes, for example, should normally be bright and alert, so if the haw is bloodshot or partially covers the eye, it may be a sign of illness or irritation. If your dog has matter in the corners of his eyes, bathe them with a mild eye wash; obtain ointment or eye drops from your veterinarian to treat a chronic condition.

If your dog seems to have something wrong with his ears which causes him to scratch at them or shake his head, cautiously probe the ear with a cotton swab. An accumulation of wax will probably work itself out. Dirt or dried blood, however, is indicative of ear mites or infection and should be treated immediately. Sore ears in the summer, due to insect bites, should be washed with mild soap and water, then covered with a soothing ointment and wrapped in gauze if necessary. Keep your pet away from insects until his ears heal, even if this means confining him indoors.

INOCULATIONS

Periodic check-ups by your veterinarian throughout your puppy's life is good health insurance. The person from whom your puppy was purchased should tell you what inoculations your puppy has had and when the next visit to the vet is necessary.

An Elizabethan collar can be made by cutting a piece of heavy cardboard, as shown. Its purpose is to keep your dog from scratching a head wound or a suture.

You must make certain that your puppy has been vaccinated against the following infectious canine

Unless treated promptly, the disease goes into advanced stages with infections of the lungs, intestines, and nervous

diseases: distemper, canine hepatitis, leptospirosis, rabies, parvovirus, and parainfluenza. Annual "boosters" thereafter provide inexpensive protection for your dog against such serious diseases. Puppies should also be checked for worms at an early age.

Provide your dog with a nutritional, balanced diet and opportunities for daily exercise to keep his skeletal structure healthy and strong.

DISTEMPER

Young dogs are most susceptible to distemper, although it may affect dogs of all ages. Signs of the disease are loss of appetite, depression, chills, and fever, as well as a watery discharge from the eyes and nose.

system. Dogs that recover may be impaired with paralysis, convulsions, a twitch, or some other defect, usually spastic in nature. Early inoculations in puppyhood should be followed by an annual booster to help protect against this disease.

CANINE HEPATITIS

The initial symptoms of hepatitis are drowsiness, vomiting, loss of appetite, high temperature, and great thirst. Often these symptoms are accompanied by swellings of the head, neck, and abdomen. This disease strikes quickly, and death may occur in only a few hours. An annual booster shot is needed after the initial series of puppy shots.

LEPTOSPIROSIS

Infection is begun by the dog's licking substances contaminated by the urine or feces of infected animals, and the disease is carried by bacteria that live in stagnant or slow-moving water. The symptoms are diarrhea and a yellowish-brownish discoloration of the jaws, teeth, and tongue, caused by an inflammation of the kidneys. A veterinarian can administer the leptospirosis shot along with the distemper and hepatitis shot.

RABIES

This disease of the dog's central nervous system spreads by infectious saliva which is transmitted by the bite of an infected animal. Of the two main classes of symptoms, the first is "furious rabies," in which the dog shows a period of melancholy or depression, then irritation, and finally paralysis. The first period can be from a few hours to several days, and during this time the dog is cross and will change his position often, lose his appetite, begin to lick, and bite or swallow foreign

objects. During this phase the dog is spasmodically wild and has impulses to run away. The dog acts fearless and bites everything in sight. If he is caged or confined, he will fight at the bars and possibly break teeth or fracture his jaw. His bark becomes a peculiar howl. In the final stage, the animal's lower jaw becomes paralyzed and hangs down. He then walks with a stagger, and saliva drips from his mouth. About four to eight

The stifle, or knee joint, is in the dog's hind leg and is formed by the articulation of the upper and lower thighs.

days after the onset of paralysis, the dog dies.

The second class of symptoms is referred to as "dumb rabies" and is characterized by the dog's walking in a bearlike manner with his head down. The lower jaw is paralyzed and the dog is unable to bite. It appears as if he has a bone caught in his throat.

health department must be notified in the case of a rabid dog, for this is a danger to all who come near him. As with the other shots each year, an annual rabies inoculation is very important. In many areas, the administration of rabies vaccines for dogs is required by law.

Dorsal view of the canine heart.

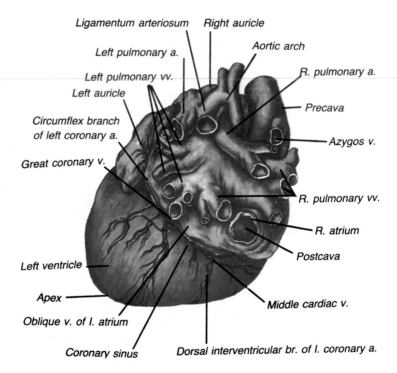

Ligamentum arteriosum
Left pulmonary a.
Left pulmonary vv.
Left auricle
Circumflex branch of left coronary a.
Great coronary v.
Right auricle
Aortic arch
R. pulmonary a.
Precava
Azygos v.
R. pulmonary vv.
R. atrium
Postcava
Left ventricle
Apex
Oblique v. of l. atrium
Coronary sinus
Middle cardiac v.
Dorsal interventricular br. of l. coronary a.

If a dog is bitten by a rabid animal, he probably can be saved if he is taken to a veterinarian in time for a series of injections. After the symptoms appear, however, no cure is possible. The local

PARVOVIRUS

This relatively new virus is a contagious disease that has spread in almost epidemic proportions throughout certain sections of the United States. Also, it has appeared

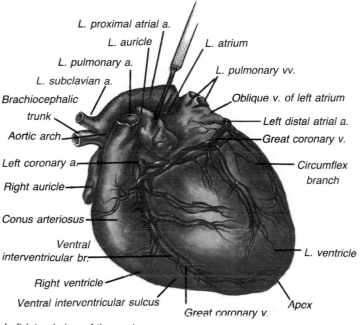

L. proximal atrial a.

L. auricle

L. atrium

L. pulmonary a.

L. pulmonary vv.

L. subclavian a.

Brachiocephalic trunk

Oblique v. of left atrium

Aortic arch

Left distal atrial a.

Great coronary v.

Left coronary a.

Circumflex branch

Right auricle

Conus arteriosus

Ventral interventricular br.

L. ventricle

Right ventricle

Ventral interventricular sulcus

Great coronary v.

Apex

Left lateral view of the canine heart.

in Australia, Canada, and Europe. Canine parvovirus attacks the intestinal tract, white blood cells, and heart muscle. It is believed to spread through dog-to-dog contact, and the specific course of infection seems to come from fecal matter of infected dogs. Overcoming parvovirus is difficult, for it is capable of existing in the environment for many months under varying conditions and temperatures, and it can be transmitted from place to place on the hair and feet of infected dogs, as well as on the clothes and shoes of people.

Vomiting and severe diarrhea, which will appear within five to seven days after the animal has been exposed to the virus, are the initial signs of this disease. At the onset of illness, feces will be light gray or yellow-gray in color, and the urine might be blood-streaked. Because of the vomiting and severe diarrhea, the dog that has contracted the disease will dehydrate quickly. Depression and loss of appetite, as well as a rise in temperature, can accompany the other symptoms. Death caused by this disease usually occurs within 48 to 72 hours following the appearance of the symptoms. Puppies are hardest hit, and the virus is fatal to 75 percent of puppies that contract it. Death in puppies can be within two

95

days of the onset of the illness.

A series of shots administered by a veterinarian is the best preventive measure for canine parvovirus. It is also important to disinfect the area where the dog is housed by using

Your local pet shop can advise you on which type of shampoo best suits the needs of your dog. If he is plagued with fleas or ticks, there are special preparations available.

one part sodium hypochlorite solution (household bleach) to thirty parts of water and to keep the dog from coming into contact with the fecal matter of other dogs.

PARAINFLUENZA

Parainfluenza, or infectious canine tracheobronchitis, is commonly known as "kennel cough." It is highly contagious, affects the upper respiratory system, and is spread through direct or indirect contact with already diseased dogs. It will readily infect dogs of all ages that have not been vaccinated or that were previously infected. While this condition is definitely one of the serious diseases in dogs, it is self-limiting, usually lasting only

two to four weeks. The symptoms are high fever and intense, harsh coughing that brings up mucus. As long as your pet sees your veterinarian immediately, the chances for his complete recovery are excellent.

EXTERNAL PARASITES

A parasite is an animal that lives in or on an organism of another species known as the host. The majority of dogs' skin problems are parasitic in nature and an estimated 90% of puppies are born with parasites.

Ticks can cause serious problems to dogs where the

In the top photo, the gums appear healthy and the tooth surfaces are relatively clean, while in the lower photo, the gums are moderately to severely inflamed and a great deal of plaque and calculus are present. These photos serve to illustrate the importance of canine dental care. Photos courtesy of Dr. J. Hock, School of Dental Medicine, University of Connecticut.

latter have access to woods, fields, and vegetation in which large numbers of native mammals live. Ticks are usually found clinging to vegetation and attach themselves to animals passing by. They have eight legs and a heavy shield or shell-like covering on their upper surface. Only by keeping dogs away from tick-infested areas can ticks on dogs be prevented.

The flea is the single most common cause of skin and coat problems in dogs. There are 11,000 kinds of fleas

The common dog flea, magnified a great number of times. If your dog has fleas, not only will you have to treat him, but you will have to treat his entire environment as well; in other words, you will have to attack on two fronts.

A greatly magnified drawing of a tick. Check your dog's coat often for these pesky parasites, particularly during the warm-weather months.

which can transmit specific disorders like tapeworm and heartworm or transport smaller parasites onto your dog. The common tapeworm, for example, requires the flea as an intermediate host for completion of its life cycle. A female flea can lay hundreds of eggs and these will become adults in less than three weeks. Depending on the temperature and the amount

of moisture, large numbers of fleas can attack dogs, and the ears of dogs, in particular, can play host to hundreds of fleas.

Fleas can lurk in crevices and cracks, carpets, and bedding for months, so frequent cleaning of your dog's environment is absolutely essential. If he is infected by other dogs, then have him bathed and "dipped," which means that he will be put into water containing a chemical that kills fleas. Your veterinarian will advise which dip to use and your dog must be bathed.

These parasites are tenacious and remarkably agile creatures; fleas have existed since prehistoric times and have been found in arctic as well as tropical climates. Some experts claim that fleas can jump 150 times the length of their bodies; this makes them difficult to catch and kill.

Thus, treating your pet for parasites without simultaneously treating the environment is both inefficient and ineffective.

INTERNAL PARASITES

Four common internal parasites that may infect a dog are: roundworms, hookworms, whipworms, and tapeworms. The first three can be diagnosed by laboratory examination of the dog's stool, and tapeworms can be determined by seeing segments in the stool or attached to the hair around the anus. When a veterinarian determines what type of worm or worms are present, he then can advise the best treatment.

Roundworms, the dog's most common intestinal parasite, have a life cycle which permits complete eradication by worming twice, ten days apart. The first worming will remove all adults and the second will destroy all subsequently hatched eggs

This is the mite that causes red mange. Here it is enlarged, but in reality it is microscopic.

The sarcoptic mange mite burrows into the dog's skin where it creates havoc. Sarcoptic mange is contagious, and young pups are especially susceptible.

before they, in turn, can produce more parasites.

A dog in good physical condition is less susceptible to worm infestation than a weak dog. Proper sanitation and a nutritious diet help in preventing worms. One of the best preventive measures is to have clean, dry bedding for the dog, as this diminishes the possibility of reinfection due to flea or tick bites.

Heartworm infestation in dogs is passed by mosquitoes. Dogs with this disease tire easily, have difficulty in breathing, and lose weight despite a hearty appetite. Administration of preventive medicine throughout the spring, summer, and fall months is advised. A veterinarian must first take a blood sample from the dog to test for the presence of the disease, and if the dog is heartworm-free, pills or liquid medicine can be prescribed to protect against any infestation.

CANINE SENIOR CITIZENS

The processes of aging and gradual degenerative changes start far earlier in a dog than often observed, usually at about seven years of age. If we recall that each year of a dog's life roughly corresponds to about seven years in the life of a man, by the age of seven he is well into middle age. Your pet will become less active, will have a poorer appetite with increased thirst, there will be frequent periods of constipation and less than normal passage of urine. His skin and coat might become dull and dry and his hair will become thin and fall out. There is a tendency towards obesity in old age, which should be avoided by maintaining a regular exercise program. Remember, also, that your pet will be less able to cope with extreme heat,

cold, fatigue, and change in routine.

There is the possibility of loss or impairment of hearing or eyesight. He may become bad-tempered more often

than in the past. Other ailments such as rheumatism, arthritis, kidney infections, heart disease, male prostatism, and hip dysplasia may occur. Of course, all these require a veterinarian's examination and recommendation of suitable treatment. Care of the teeth is also important in the aging dog. Indeed, the mouth can be a barometer of nutritional health. Degenerating gums, heavy tartar on the teeth, loose teeth, and sore lips are common. The worst of all diseases in old age, however, is neglect. Good care in early life will have its effect on your dog's later years; the nutrition and general health care of his first few years can determine his lifespan and the quality of his life. It is worth bearing in mind that the older, compared to the younger, animal needs more protein of good biological value, more vitamins A, B-complex, D and

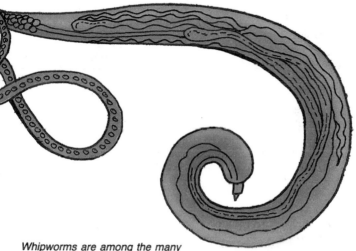

Whipworms are among the many internal parasites that can attack dogs. Your veterinarian is best qualified to detect the presence of worms, if they exist, in your dog.

E, more calcium and iron, less fat and fewer carbohydrates.

The companionship of pets, not only to children and adults, but particularly to the aged and lonely, cannot be overestimated. Therefore, a dog's grateful owner should do all he can to enhance and prolong the life of his cherished companion. Regular doses of TLC or Tender Loving Care is the best "medicine" your dog can receive throughout his life.

DEATH OF A FRIEND

What can you do, however, for a pet who is so sick or severely injured that he will never recover his normal health? Although one is often extremely reluctant to consider the suggestion, sometimes the kindest and most humane solution is to have your veterinarian put him out of his misery by inducing his death peacefully and painlessly. This process is called euthanasia, a word of Greek derivation meaning "easy or good death." It is usually carried out by having your veterinarian inject a death-inducing drug or an overdose of anesthetic.

Such a decision will probably be an extremely difficult one for you to make but you need not, in fact, should not, make it alone.

Your veterinarian should be your chief adviser and family and friends can assist in the decision-making process. Your children should not be excluded from this painful time; it would be inadvisable to attempt to "shield" or "protect" them from such events which are an inevitable part of life. They would suffer even more if, later, they did not understand how or why their beloved pet had died.

memories. People who do not have pets often fail to realize what a very important part of our lives these animals fill and what a void is created by their absence. Others are more sympathetic and compassionate. Rest assured,

Digestive action usually slows down as your dog ages, so check with your veterinarian about your canine senior citizen's special dietary needs.

CANINE DIGESTIVE APPARATUS

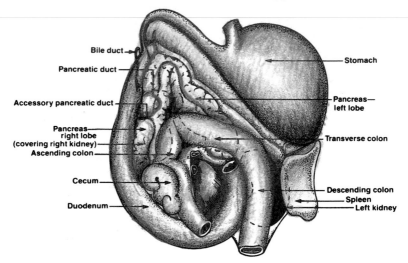

By remembering the wonderful times with your pet, by talking about him to family and friends, by remembering him as healthy and full of life, you will eventually cope with your grief. It is perfectly natural to grieve for the loss of such a loyal, affectionate companion who has provided you with so many happy

however, that if you have chosen a painless, eternal sleep for your pet by "putting him to sleep" (an appropriate euphemism in this case), you have done him a final service as a loving, considerate friend.

Breeding

If you own a bitch and you want to breed her, first make sure you can handle the responsibility of caring for her and her litter of pups. Consider the time and money involved just to get her into breeding condition and then to sustain her throughout pregnancy and afterwards while she tends her young. You will be obligated to house, feed, groom, and housebreak the puppies until good homes can be found for them; and, lest we forget, there will be periodic trips to the vet for check-ups, wormings, and inoculations. Common sense should tell you that it is indeed cruel to bring unwanted or unplanned puppies into an already crowded canine world; only negligent pet owners allow this to happen. With pet-quality purebred dogs, most breeders require prospective pet owners to sign a neuter/spay agreement when they purchase their dogs. In this way breeders can be assured that only their very best stock of show-quality and breeder-quality animals, *i.e.,* those that match closely their individual standards of perfection and those that are free of genetic disorders or disease, will be used to propagate the breed.

Before you select a stud to mate with your bitch, think carefully about why you want her to give birth to a litter of puppies. If you feel she will be deprived in some way if she is

Anatomy of the dog's foot. Infections between the toes are quite common in the older dog. as he tends to have a lowered resistance to disease, less vitality, and a less active circulation. This is why it is important to check your aging dog's feet regularly.

not bred, if you think your children will learn from the experience, if you have the mistaken notion that you will make money from this great undertaking, think again. A dog can lead a perfectly happy, healthy, normal life without having been mated; in fact, spaying a female and neutering a male help them become better pets, as they are not so anxious to search for a mate in an effort to relieve their sexual tensions. As for giving the children a lesson in sex education, this is hardly a valid reason for breeding your dog. And on an economic level, it takes not only years of hard work (researching pedigrees and bloodlines, studying genetics, among other things), but it takes plenty of capital (money, equipment, facilities) to make a decent profit from dog breeding. Why most dedicated breeders are lucky just to break even. If you have

THE FEMALE "IN SEASON"

A bitch may come into season (also known as "heat" or estrus) once or several times a year, depending on the particular breed and the individual dog. Her first seasonal period, that is to say, the time when she is capable of being fertilized by a male dog, may occur as early as six months with some breeds. If you own a female and your intention is *not* to

A profile and frontal view of the scissors bite, in which the lower teeth touch the inside of the upper teeth.

only a casual interest in dog breeding, it is best to leave this pastime to those who are more experienced in such matters, those who consider it a serious hobby or vocation. If you have bought a breeder— or show-quality canine, one that may be capable of producing champions, and if you are just starting out with this breeding venture, seek advice from the seller of your dog, from other veteran breeders, and from your veterinarian before you begin.

breed her, by all means discuss with the vet the possibility of having her spayed: this means before she reaches sexual maturity.

The first sign of the female's being in season is a thin red discharge, which may increase for about a week; it then changes color to a thin yellowish stain, which lasts about another week. Simultaneously, there is a swelling of the vulva, the exterior portion of the female's reproductive tract; the soft, flabby vulva indicates her readiness to mate.

Mitosis, or cell division, beginning. The chromosomes (top left) are becoming thicker and more obvious in the cell's nucleus. The spindle, a web of fibers, forms (top right) and covers the middle of the cell. The nucleus disappears and the chromosomes split and are pulled to opposite sides of the cell. (Below) the cell has almost divided into two.

Around this second week or so ovulation occurs, and this is the crucial period for her to be bred, if this is what you have in mind for her. It is during this middle phase of the heat cycle when conception can take place. Just remember that there is great variation from bitch to bitch with regard to how often they come into heat, how long the heat cycles last, how long the period of ovulation lasts, and how much time elapses between heat cycles. Generally, after the third week of heat, the vulval swelling decreases and the estrus period ceases for several months.

It should be mentioned that the female will probably lose her puppy coat, or at least shed part of it, about three months after she has come into season. This is the time when her puppies would have been weaned, had she been mated, and females generally drop coat at this time.

With female dogs, there are few, if any, behavioral changes during estrus. A bitch may dart out of an open door to greet all available male dogs that show an interest in her, and she may occasionally raise her tail and assume a mating stance, particularly if you pet her lower back; but these signs are not as dramatic as those of the sexually mature male. He himself does not experience heat cycles;

Three types of bites seen in dogs: top, scissors; middle, overshot; and bottom, undershot.

rather, he is attracted to the female during all phases of her seasonal period. He usually becomes more aggressive and tends to fight with other males, especially over females in heat. He tends to mark his territory with urine to attract females and at the same time to warn other competitive males. It is not uncommon to see him mount various objects, and people, in an effort to satisfy his mature sexual urges.

If you are a homeowner and you have an absolutely climb-proof and dig-proof run within your yard, it may be safe to leave your bitch in season there. But then again it may not be a wise idea, as there have been cases of males mating with females right through chain-link fencing! Just to be on the safe side, shut her indoors during her heat periods and don't let her outdoors until you are certain the estrus period is over. Never leave a bitch in heat outdoors, unsupervised, even for a minute so that she can defecate or urinate. If you want to prevent the neighborhood dogs from hanging around your doorstep, as they inevitably will do when they discover your female is in season, take her some distance away from the house before you let her do her business. Otherwise, these canine suitors will be attracted to her by the arousing odor of her urine, and they will know instinctively that she isn't far from her scented "calling card." If you need to walk your bitch, take her in the car to a nearby park or field for a chance to stretch her legs. Remember that after about three weeks, and this varies from dog to dog, you can let her outdoors again with no

(vacations, business trips, social engagements, and so on). Make sure you will be able to set aside plenty of

Ext. iliac a. & v.

R. uterine horn

Ovary

Wing of sacrum

Postcava

Colon

Vagina

Bladder

Urethra

The female dog's reproductive system. When all goes well for a bitch during pregnancy, all of the reproductive organs work together in harmony.
(a. = artery; v. = vein; r. = right; Ext. = external).

worry that she can have puppies until the next heat period.

WHEN TO BREED

It is usually best to breed a bitch when she comes into her second or third season. Plan in advance the time of year which is best for you, taking into account your own schedule of activities

time to assist with whelping of the newborn pups and caring for the dam and her litter for the next few weeks. At the very least, it probably will take an hour or so each day just to feed and clean up after the brood—but undoubtedly you will find it takes much longer if you stop to admire and play with the youngsters periodically! Refrain from selling the litter until it is at least six weeks old, keeping in mind that a litter of pups takes up a fair amount of

Hopefully, as strongly recommended, you will have already lined up buyers for the pups in advance of their arrival into this world.

Pelvic urethra

Body of penis

Region of bulbus glandis

Prepuce

Ext. pudendal

The male dog's reproductive system. (Ext. = external).

space by then. It will be your responsibility to provide for them until they have been weaned from their mother, properly socialized, housebroken, and ready to go to new homes (unless you plan to keep them all).

CHOOSING THE STUD

You can plan to breed your female about six-and-one-half months after the start of her last season, although a variation of a month or two either way is not unusual. Do some research into the various bloodlines within your breed and then choose a stud dog and make arrangements well in advance. If you are breeding for show stock, which will command higher prices than pet-quality animals, a mate should be chosen very carefully. He should complement any deficiencies (bad traits) that your female may have, and he should have a good show record or be the sire of show winners, if he is old enough to have proven himself. If possible, the bitch and stud should have several ancestors in common within the last two or three generations, as such combinations have been known, generally, to "click" best.

The owner of a stud dog usually charges a stud fee for use of the animal's services. This does not always guarantee a litter, but if she fails to conceive, chances are

Although full dentition is most desirable in show dogs, it is not uncommon to find dogs with missing teeth.

you may be able to breed your female to that stud again. In some instances the owner of the stud will agree to take a "first pick of the litter" in place of a fee. You should, of course, settle all details beforehand, including the possibility of a single puppy surviving, deciding the age at which the pup is to be taken, and so forth.

If you plan to raise a litter that will be sold exclusively as pets, and if you merely plan to make use of an available male (not a top stud dog), the most important selection point involves temperament. Make sure the dog is friendly, as well as healthy, because a bad disposition can be passed on to his puppies— and this is the worst of all traits in a dog destined to be a pet. If you are breeding pet-quality dogs, a "stud fee puppy," not necessarily the choice of the litter, is the usual payment. Don't breed indiscriminately; be sure you will be able to find good homes for each of the pups, or be sure you have the

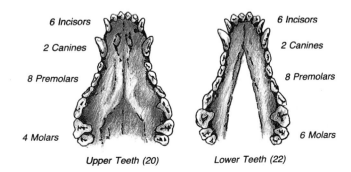

6 Incisors

2 Canines

8 Premolars

4 Molars

6 Incisors

2 Canines

8 Premolars

6 Molars

Upper Teeth (20)   Lower Teeth (22)

Correct Dentition

facilities to keep them yourself, *before* you plan to mate your dog.

PREPARATION FOR BREEDING

Before you breed your female, make sure she is in good health. She should be neither too thin nor too fat. Any skin disease *must* be cured first so that it is not passed on to the puppies. If she has worms, she should be wormed before being bred or within three weeks after the mating. It is generally considered a good idea to revaccinate her against distemper and hepatitis before the puppies are born. This will increase the immunity the puppies receive during their early, most vulnerable period.

The female will probably be ready to breed twelve days after the first colored discharge appears. You can usually make arrangements to board her with the owner of the stud for a few days, to insure her being there at the proper time; or you can take her to be mated and bring her home the same day if you live near enough to the stud's owner. If the bitch still appears receptive she may be bred again two days later, just to make certain the mating was successful. However, some females never show signs of willingness, so it helps to have an experienced breeder on hand. In fact, you both may have to assist with

Facing page: lifecycle of a dog tapeworm. Fleas swallow tapeworm eggs which develop into larvae inside them. When a dog eats an infected flea, the larvae transform into the head (or scolex) of the adult tapeworm. The scolex attaches to the dog's intestinal lining and develops egg-containing segments that are passed out with the dog's feces, and the cycle continues.

the mating by holding the animals against each other to ensure the "tie" is not broken, that is, to make certain copulation takes place. Sometimes, too, you'll need to muzzle the bitch to keep her from biting you or the stud.

Usually the second day after the discharge changes color is the proper time to mate the bitch, and she may be bred for about three days following this time. For an additional week or so, she may have some discharge and attract other dogs by her odor; but she should not be bred. Once she has been bred, keep her far from all other male dogs, as they have the capacity to impregnate her again and sire some of her puppies. This could prove disastrous where purebred puppies—especially show-quality ones—are concerned.

THE FEMALE IN WHELP

You can expect the puppies nine weeks from the day of the mating, although sixty-one days is as common as sixty-three. Gestation, that period

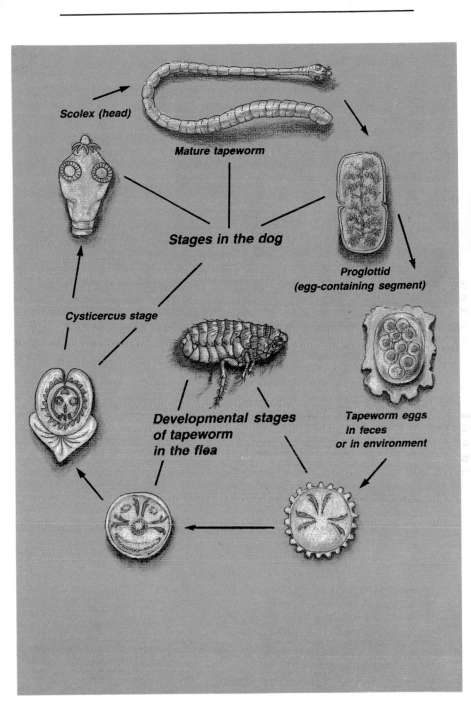

Scolex (head)

Mature tapeworm

Stages in the dog

Proglottid
(egg-containing segment)

Cysticercus stage

Developmental stages
of tapeworm
in the flea

Tapeworm eggs
in feces
or in environment

when the pups are developing inside their mother, varies among individual bitches. During this time the female should receive normal care and exercise. If she was overweight at the start, don't increase her food right away; excess weight at whelping time can be a problem with some dogs. If she is on the thin side, however, supplement her meal or meals with a portion of milk and biscuit at noontime. This will help build her up and put weight on her.

You may want to add a mineral and vitamin supplement to her diet, on the advice of your veterinarian, since she will need an extra supply not only for herself but for the puppies growing inside

mother will have little room for food and less of an appetite. She should be tempted with meat, liver, and milk, however.

As the female in whelp grows heavier, cut out violent exercise and jumping from her usual routine. Although a dog used to such activities will often play with the children or run around voluntarily, restrain her for her own sake.

A sign that whelping is imminent is the loss of hair around her breasts. This is nature's way of "clearing a path" so that the puppies will be able to find their source of nourishment. As parturition

Vitamins and minerals are a vital part of the pregnant bitch's diet.

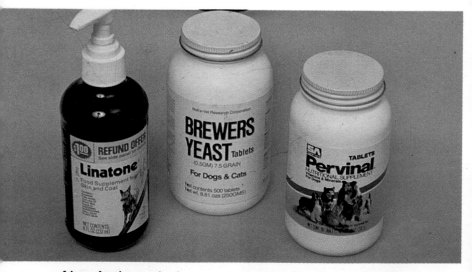

of her. As the mother's appetite increases, feed her more. During the last two weeks of pregnancy, the pups grow enormously and the

draws near, the breasts will have swelled with milk and the nipples will have enlarged and darkened to a rosy pink. If the hair in the breast region does

Fertilization is the union of two special cells, the egg from the female and the sperm from the male. One of these sperm has penetrated the membrane that surrounds the egg.

such as a corner of your cellar or garage (provided these places are warm and dry). An unused room, such as a dimly

not shed for some reason, you can easily cut it short with a pair of scissors or comb it out so that it does not mat and become a hindrance to the suckling pups later on.

PREPARING FOR THE PUPPIES

Prepare a whelping box a few days before the puppies are due, and allow the mother to sleep there overnight or to spend some time in it during the day to become accustomed to it. Then she is less likely to try to have her pups under the front porch or in the middle of your bed. A variety of places will serve,

lit spare bedroom, can also serve as the place for delivery. If the weather is warm, a large outdoor dog house will do, as long as it is well protected from rain, drafts, and the cold—and enclosed by fencing or a run. A whelping box serves to separate mother and puppies from visitors and other distractions. The walls should be high enough to restrain the puppies yet low enough to allow the mother to take a short respite from her brood after she has fed them. Four feet square is minimum size (for most dogs) and six-to-eight-inch high walls will keep the pups in until they begin to climb; then side walls should be built up so that the young ones cannot wander away from their nest. As the puppies grow, they really need more room anyway, so double the space with a very low partition down the middle of the box, and soon you will find them naturally housebreaking themselves. Puppies rarely relieve themselves where they sleep.

Layers of newspapers spread over the whole area will make excellent bedding and be absorbent enough to keep the surface warm and dry. These should be removed daily and replaced with another thick layer. An old quilt or washable blanket makes better footing for the nursing puppies than slippery newspaper during the first week; this is also softer for the mother to lie on.

Be prepared for the actual whelping several days in advance. Usually the mother will tear up papers, refuse food, and become restless. These may be false alarms; the real test is her temperature, which will drop to below 100°F about twelve hours before whelping. Take her temperature with a rectal thermometer, morning and evening, and usher her to her whelping box when her temperature goes down. Keep a close watch on her and make sure she stays safely indoors (or outdoors in a safe enclosure); if she is let

Dog breeders usually keep a sterilized pair of scissors handy in case they need to cut a puppy's umbilical cord during whelping.

outside, unleashed, or allowed to roam freely, she could wander off and start to go into labor. It is possible that she could whelp anywhere and this could be unfortunate if she needs your assistance.

WHELPING

Usually little help is needed from you, but it is wise to stay close to make sure that the mother's lack of experience (if this is her first time) does not cause an unnecessary complication. Be ready to help when the first puppy arrives, for it could smother if she does not break the amniotic membrane enclosing it. She should tear open the sac and start licking the puppy, drying and stimulating it. Check to see that all fluids have been cleared from the pup's nostrils and mouth after the mother has licked her youngster clean; otherwise, the pup may have difficulty breathing. If the mother fails to tear open the sac and stimulate the newborn's breathing, you can do this yourself by tearing the sac with your hands and then gently rubbing the infant with a soft, rough towel. The afterbirth, attached to the puppy by the long umbilical cord, should follow the birth of each puppy. Watch to make sure that each afterbirth is expelled, for the retaining of this material can cause infection. In her instinct for

stimulate her milk supply, as well as labor, for remaining pups. But eating too many afterbirths can make her lose appetite for the food she needs to feed her pups and regain her strength. So remove the rest of them, along with the wet newspapers, and keep the box dry and clean.

If the mother does not bite the cord, or bites it too close to the puppy's body, take over the job to prevent an umbilical hernia. Tearing is recommended; but you can

Whelping boxes can be constructed of smooth wood. Make sure you include a "pig rail" around the inside perimeter of the box to keep the mother from crushing her pups.

cleanliness the mother will probably eat the afterbirth after severing the umbilical cord. One or two meals of this will not hurt her; they

cut the cord, about two inches from the body, with a sawing motion of scissors that have been sterilized in alcohol. Then dip the end of the cut cord in a shallow dish of iodine; the cord will dry up and fall off in a few days.

The puppies may follow each other in a few minutes or a few hours, as the time varies with each bitch. If she is actively straining without producing a puppy, the youngster may be presented backward, a so-called "breech" birth. Careful assistance with a well-lubricated finger to feel for the puppy or ease it back may help, but never attempt to pull it out by force. This could cause serious damage, so seek the services of an expert—your veterinarian or an experienced breeder.

If *anything* seems wrong, during labor or parturition, waste no time in calling your veterinarian who can examine the bitch and, if necessary, give her hormones to stimulate the birth of the remaining puppies. You may want his experience in whelping the litter even if all goes well. He will probably prefer to have the puppies

The shoulder and arm musculature. Unless your dog has suffered a serious injury or was born with a congenital defect, his bones, muscles, and joints should remain healthy until he reaches middle age— around five or six years old.

born at his hospital rather than to get up in the middle of the night to come to your home. The mother would, no doubt, prefer to stay at home; but you can be sure she will get the best of care in a veterinary hospital. If the puppies are born at home and all goes as it should, watch the mother carefully afterward. Within a day or two of the birth, it is wise to have the veterinarian check her and the pups to ensure all is well.

Make sure each puppy finds a teat and starts nursing right away, as these first few meals supply colostral antibodies to help the pup fight disease. As soon as he is dry, hold each puppy to a nipple for a good meal without competition. Then he may join his littermates in the whelping box, out of his mother's way while she continues giving birth. Keep a supply of evaporated milk on hand for emergency feedings or later weaning. A formula of evaporated milk, corn syrup, and a little water with egg yolk should be warmed and fed in a doll's or baby's bottle if necessary. Or purchase a pet nurser kit to have on hand; these are available in local pet shops. A supplementary feeding often helps weak pups (those that may have difficulty nursing) over the hump. Keep track of birth weights and weekly readings thereafter; this will furnish an accurate record of the pups' growth and health, and the information will be valuable for your veterinarian.

RAISING THE PUPPIES
After the puppies have been born, take the mother outside for a walk and drink of water, and then leave her to take

care of her brood. She will probably not want to stay away more than a minute or two for the first few weeks. Be sure to keep water available at all times and feed her milk or broth frequently, as she needs liquids to produce milk. Encourage her to eat, with her favorite foods, until she seeks it of her own accord. She will soon develop a ravenous appetite and should have at least two large meals a day, with dry food available in addition. Your veterinarian can guide you on the finer points of nutrition as they apply to nursing dams.

Prepare a warm place to put the puppies after they are born to keep them dry and help them to a good start in life. An electric heating pad or hot water bottle covered with flannel can be placed in the bottom of a cardboard box and near the mother so that she can see her puppies. She will usually allow you to help her care for the youngsters, but don't take them out of her sight. Let her handle things if your interference seems to make her nervous.

Be sure that all the puppies are getting enough to eat. If

Normally the dam will cut the umbilical cord with her teeth. The short stub that remains dries up and falls off in a couple of days.

the mother sits or stands instead of lying still to nurse, the probable cause is scratching from the puppies' nails. You can remedy this by clipping them, as you would the bitch's, with a pet nail clipper. Or manicure scissors will do for these tiny claws. Some breeders advise disposing of the smaller or weaker pups in a large litter, as the mother has trouble handling more than six or seven. You can help her out by preparing an extra puppy box or basket furnished with a heating pad and some bedding material. Leave half the litter with the mother and the other half in the extra box, changing off at two-hour intervals at first. Later you may exchange them less frequently, leaving them all together except during the day. Try supplementary feedings, too; as soon as their eyes open, at about two weeks, they will lap from a small dish.

WEANING THE PUPPIES

Normally the puppies should be completely weaned at five weeks, although you can start to feed them at three weeks. They will find it easier to lap semi-solid food than to drink milk at first, so mix baby cereal with whole or evaporated milk, warmed to body temperature, and offer it to the puppies in a saucer. Until they learn to lap it, it is best to feed one or two at a time because they are more likely to walk into it than to eat it. Hold the saucer at their

chin level, and let them gather around, keeping paws out of the dish. A damp sponge afterward prevents most of the cereal from sticking to the skin if the mother doesn't clean them up. Once they have gotten the idea, broth or babies' meat soup may be alternated with milk, and you can start them on finely chopped meat. At about four weeks, they will eat four meals a day and soon do without their mother entirely. Start them on canned dog food, or leave dry puppy food with them in a dish for self-feeding. Don't leave water with them all the time; at this age everything is a play toy and they will use it as a wading pool. They can drink all they need if it is offered several times a day, after

Pet shops stock pet nurser kits for those dog owners who need to hand-feed their puppies. Such kits come complete with bottle, nipples, and bottle brush.

meals. As the puppies grow up the mother will go into their "pen" only to nurse them, first sitting up and then standing. To dry up her milk

The puppies may be put outside during the day, unless it is too cold or rainy, as soon as their eyes are open. They will benefit from the sunlight.

supply completely, keep the mother away for longer periods; after a few days of part-time nursing she can stay away for even longer periods, and then permanently. The little milk left will be resorbed by her body.

Chocolate Nylabones® and similar products are ideal for puppies. They have a very thin layer of chocolate deposited UNDER the surface of the bone. The flavor is released as the dog chews on the knuckle. The bone must be replaced when the knuckle is worn down.

A rubber mat or newspapers underneath will protect them from cold or dampness. As they mature, the pups can be let out for longer intervals, although make sure you provide them with a shelter at night or in bad weather. By now, cleaning up after the matured youngsters is a man-sized job, so put them out at least during the day and make your task easier. If you enclose them in a run or kennel, remember to clean it *daily,* as various parasites and other infectious organisms may be lurking if the quarters are kept dirty.

present. If one puppy is infected then all should be wormed as a preventive measure. Follow the veterinarian's advice; this also applies to vaccinations. If you plan to keep a pup yourself, you will want to vaccinate him, and his littermates, at the earliest age. This way, those pups destined for new homes will be protected against some of the more debilitating canine diseases.

THE DECISION TO SPAY OR NEUTER

If you decide not to use your male or female for

Puppies can be transported to the vet in carriers like this one.

You can expect the pups to need at least one worming before they are ready to go to new homes; so for each animal, before they are three weeks old, take a stool sample to your veterinarian. The vet can determine, by analyzing the stool, if any of the pups have worms—and if so, what kind of worms are

breeding, or if you are obligated to have the animal altered based on an agreement made between you and the seller, make the necessary arrangements with your veterinarian as soon as possible. The surgery involved for both males and females is relatively simple and painless: males will be castrated and females will have their ovaries and uterus removed. In both cases, the operation does not alter their personalities; you will, however, notice that males will be less likely to roam, to get into fights with other male dogs, and to mount objects and people. From a pet owner's point of view, an animal that is less anxious and less inclined to wander off in search of a mate makes a better companion.

Your veterinarian can best determine at what age neutering or spaying should be done. With a young female dog, the operation may be somewhat more involved, and as a result be more costly;

however, in the long run you will be glad you made the decision to have this done for your pet. After a night or two at the veterinarian's or an animal hospital, your bitch can be safely returned to your home. Her stitches will heal in a short time, and when they are removed, you will hardly notice her souvenir scar of the routine operation. Once she has been spayed, she no longer will be capable of having a litter of puppies.

Check with your city or town or with the local humane society for special programs that are available for pet owners. In many municipalities you can have your pet altered for just a

Tomarctus was an early ancestor of the family Canidae, which includes not only dogs, but wolves, coyotes, jackals, foxes, and other mammals.

small fee; the low price is meant to encourage pet owners to take advantage of this important means of birth control for their dogs. Pet adoption agencies and other animal welfare organizations can house only so many animals at one time, given the money, space, and other resources they have available. This is why pet owners are urged to have their pets altered, so that puppies, resulting from accidental breedings, won't end up being put to sleep as so many others have that are lost, stray, unwanted, or abandoned.

Suggested Reading

The following books, available at most pet shops and book stores, are recommended for your reading pleasure.

HOW TO SHOW YOUR OWN DOG
By Virginia Tuck Nichols
ISBN 0-87666-661-6
PS-607

You don't necessarily need a professional handler to show your dog. What you do need is some basic information about dog shows, how a champion is made, what the terms and definitions are, and how to prepare for the big day.
Hard cover, 5½" x 8½", 288 pages 136 black and white photos; 10 line illustrations

DOG BEHAVIOR
By Dr. Ian Dunbar
ISBN 0-87666-671-3
H-1016

A book intended for everyone who likes dogs and wants to understand them better as well as for anyone interested in animal behavior.
Hard cover, 5½" x 8", 223 pages 20 full-color photos, 115 black and white photos, 3 line drawings

ENCYCLOPEDIA OF DOG BREEDS
By Ernest H. Hart
ISBN 0-87666-285-8
H-927

This comprehensive volume includes everything you need to know about feeding, basic dog training, dog diseases and first aid, and showing. All of the various dog groups are covered in depth.
Hard cover, 5½" x 8½", 784 pages 537 black and white photos; 138 color photos

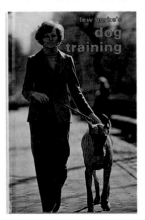

DOG TRAINING
By Lew Burke
ISBN 0-87666-656-X
H-962

The elements of dog training are easy to grasp and apply, and this guide is for dog owners age 14 and older who are anxious to discover the secrets behind Lew Burke's methods.
Hard cover, 5½" x 8½", 255 pages 64 black and white photos, 23 full-color photos

DOG OWNER'S VETERINARY GUIDE
By G. W. Stamm
ISBN 0-87666-402-8
AP-927

The most accurate and up-to-date book based on recent information set forth by various notable veterinarians.
Hard cover, 5½" x 8", 112 pages 28 black and white photos, 39 line drawings

DOG BREEDING FOR PROFESSIONALS
By Dr. Herbert Richards
ISBN 0-87666-659-4
H-969

For dog owners who need and actively seek advice about how to go about breeding their dogs either for profit or purely because of their attachment to their animals. *Please note:* This book contains highly explicit photos of canine sexual activities that some readers may find offensive.
Hard cover, 5½ x 8½", 224 pages 105 black and white photos, 62 full-color photos, 4 charts

breeding techniques, the selection of breeding partners, the importance of pedigrees, and environment and heredity are just some of the topics given ample treatment.
Hard cover, 5½ x 8½", 224 pages 77 black and white photos, 52 full-color photos

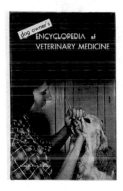

DOG BREEDING
By Ernest H. Hart
ISBN 0-87666-654-3
H-958

Easily understood and written for the breeder who is attempting to upgrade the quality of his representatives of a breed, this book covers every important aspect of breeding dogs, including both theory and completely practical day-to-day concerns. The physiology of the bitch and stud dog, gestation, whelping, fertility problems, how to build a strain,

DOG OWNER'S ENCYCLOPEDIA OF VETERINARY MEDICINE
By Allan H. Hart, B.V.Sc.
ISBN 0-87666-287-4
H-934

Written by a veterinarian who feels that most dog owners should recognize the symptoms and understand the cures of most diseases of dogs so that they can properly communicate with their veterinarian.
Hard cover, 5½" x 8", 186 pages 86 black and white photos

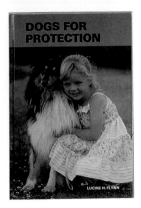

THE COMPLETE DOG BUYERS' GUIDE
By Dr. William R. Bruette and Kerry V. Donnelly
ISBN 0-86622-026-7
H-1061

In one compact volume breeders, pet owners and other dog fanciers will find complete descriptions and information about many of the world's most popular dogs—over 120 breeds are listed! Each breed is fully described as to its history and development and is illustrated. The text includes a special pricing guide for the potential dog buyer. A great book for all dog lovers—invaluable for anyone looking for good advice about which breed to obtain.
Hard cover, 5½ x 8"; 608 pages
Contains 147 black and white photos

DOGS FOR PROTECTION
By Lucine H. Flynn
ISBN 0-87666-813-9
PS-802

This book contains detailed information about choosing a dog to provide protection and about training dogs in the basic obedience routines that every protection dog must know. The author, a recognized expert in obedience teaching and judging, outlines step-by-step exercises for training a dog to be protective and alert, but not a snarling beast. This is a very practical volume.
Hard cover, 5½ x 8", 96 pages
41 full-color photos, 29 black and white photos

The Complete Dog Buyers' Guide

NEW REVISED EXPANDED

Which dog to buy? This is the only book which provides all the facts you need: standards, prices, suitability and temperament of each dog plus EVERYTHING you need to know about dog care. Covers more breeds than any other book.

ILLUSTRATED TEXTBOOK OF DOG DISEASES
By The TV Vet
ISBN 0-87666-733-7
PS-770

For all dog owners, whether your pet is purebred or a mixed breed, who want general advice about how to keep their dogs healthy.
Hard cover, 5½" x8", 284 pages
380 black and white photos, 24 color photos